TWENTY QUESTIONS ABOUT
HEALING

Also by Morris Maddocks and published by SPCK:

The Christian Healing Ministry (SPCK 1981)

Twenty Questions about Healing

MORRIS MADDOCKS

First published in Great Britain 1988
S P C K
Holy Trinity Church
Marylebone Road
London NW1 4DU

Third impression 1992

British Library Cataloguing in Publication Data

Maddocks, Morris
    Twenty questions about healing
    1. Christian life. Faith.
    I. Title
    248.4

    ISBN 0–281–04353–1

Typeset by Inforum Ltd, Portsmouth
Printed and bound in Great Britain by
BPCC Hazells Ltd
Member of BPCC Ltd

Contents

Acknowledgements

I am personally grateful to Dr Peter Nixon, Consultant Cardiologist at Charing Cross Hospital, not only for his friendship and support in the work over several years, but also for permission to use his diagram of the Human Function Curve and to quote from his teaching, some of which is used in an excellent manual on Stress by Dr Sarah Horsman. I am also grateful to my Editor at SPCK, Judith Longman, for her valuable suggestions to improve the manuscript.

The quotations from the Bible are taken from the New International Version, copyright © 1973, 1978, 1984 by International Bible Society, first published in Great Britain in 1979, and are used by permission of Hodder & Stoughton.

+ Morris Maddocks

PREFACE

The Church is sometimes accused of answering the questions no-one is asking. In this present little book, all the questions are 'live' questions: they are ones which I have been asked, some of them many times, during seminars up and down the country. My experience over the last two decades is that people are full of questions but too rarely get the opportunity to ask them. They want to know how the Christian faith affects them personally, deeply and inwardly. The healing dimension of Christianity has therefore much to say to them.

If we have hitherto made the faith chiefly cerebral, then we have been guilty of degutting it. Of course there was plenty to exercise the mind in the teaching of Jesus, but always with his mind-blowing teaching went a body-healing touch. His proclamation consisted not only of teaching and preaching, but also of healing. The teach/heal methodology of Jesus must also be ours.

From the amount and variety of questions I have met over these past years, I believe this is the gut feeling of Christians, a feeling that the faith is something to be experienced and not merely absorbed with the mind. And of course they are right.

My wife Anne and I have been blessed by our experience in the south west of England over the past four and a half years and especially by our involvement with the diocese of Bath and Wells. Peter Hancock, the adviser on healing in the diocese, has kindly made some suggestions towards the writing of this book. I am grateful for this and for the fellowship Anne and I have had with him, with John Richardson (adviser on Evangelism) and with John Woolmer (vice-chairman of the diocesan healing group) both on the job and in their homes. The whole team has received the constant support and direction of the Bishop, John Bickersteth, for which we are all deeply grateful. On a personal level, Anne and I have received much in terms of friendship and encouragement from John and Rosemary Bickersteth, as also from Tim Gregson and Mary Masters, and members of the senior staff. With all of them in mind and as a thanksgiving for Bishop John's ministry, as well as a prayer for the new ministry of Bishop George, we should like to dedicate this book as a small token of gratitude to the diocese of Bath and Wells.

+ Morris Maddocks
Feast of St Bartholomew 1987

NOTE

Readers who work their way through this book from beginning to end will find that some of the information given in the answers to earlier questions is repeated or amplified in the answers to later ones. This is for the convenience of those who wish to go straight to the questions which chiefly interest them, without having to plough through a complicated system of cross-references.

WHAT IS CHRISTIAN HEALING?

One morning on Breakfast Television I was being inter-
viewed about Christian healing. I had come with a stock
of definitions in my mind, knowing that the first ball
would be bowled fast at the middle stump, possibly a
yorker! Mercifully, we had been able to pray in the
central lobby before going into the studio. As the inter-
viewer delivered his fast ball, 'Tell me, what do you mean
by Christian healing?', I felt my mind going blank. All
the neat definitions I had thought out were wiped away,
and I heard myself saying, 'Christian healing is Jesus
Christ meeting you at the point of your need.' It was a
timely rescue by the Holy Spirit, demonstrating to me
how infinitely wiser is the wisdom of God than the
wisdom of man. Neat definitions are suspect.

Christian healing is Jesus Christ! We should pause
there for a moment, as we recognize that it is *he* who
comes to meet us at our point of need – a person, not
some quick remedy or magical formula or potent medicine. It is Jesus Christ, the Lord who heals and saves.

An encounter with him is therefore going to accomplish far more than the cure of our symptoms. When we
talk about 'healing' we usually mean 'curing'. Obviously
when we are in pain and afflicted with illness all we are
interested in is getting better, finding an immediate cure.
When we pray for someone's healing we are usually
praying for this: that God will make them well. That is a
perfectly legitimate use of prayer: intercession is standing before God on behalf of someone else. But as

Christians we know that God has a far greater blessing in store for that person, indeed for each one of us. And other blessings may be more important at that moment in the suffering person's journey than an instant cure. Though God never wills suffering, we do not need much experience of life to be aware of how greatly he uses it. After all, his own Son 'learned obedience from what he suffered and, once made perfect, he became the source of eternal salvation for all who obey him' (Hebrews 5.8f). God transformed the evil of the cross into the greatest good for humankind. But perhaps we are proceeding too far and too speedily, so let us take a look at the words used for healing in the New Testament.

There are three that are used most frequently. Of these, possibly the most important is *sōzō*, used thirty-eight times if we exclude parallel passages, eleven of which refer to physical healing or exorcism, and nine more to deliverance from death. In all these cases, however, the idea of the whole person being healed or delivered is conveyed by the verb, so that one writer can say, 'In the healings of Jesus *sōzō* never refers to a single member of the body, but always to the whole man.'[1] This is illustrated in the use of the word both at Mark 5.34, 'Your faith has *healed* you' (to the woman with the flow of blood), and also at Luke 7.50, 'Your faith has *saved* you; go in peace' (to the woman who was a sinner and not needing a physical cure). It is the *whole* person that needs salvation (*sōtēria* – derived from *sōzō*), and in the New Testament the verb always seems to refer to both the physical and the spiritual healing of the person. *Sōzō* is essentially a wholistic word. Its comprehensive use in the Gospels demonstrates how the Christian concepts of healing and salvation overlap and merge. As John Wilkinson says, 'Healing of the body is never purely

2

physical, and the salvation of the soul is never purely spiritual, but both are combined in the deliverance of the whole man' (person).[2] This word, with its connotation of wholeness, has much to teach us about Christian healing.

A second word used in the New Testament is *therapeuō*, from which we get the word 'therapeutic'. Originally it was used of rendering service to a person, and so came to be used of medical treatment, the purpose of a physician's *therapeia* (i.e. therapy) being to bring a person to health. Although the idea of therapy and treatment comes nearer to its original meaning, in the Gospels it is invariably used of the miraculous healings by Jesus, usually of physical healings, but sometimes of exorcisms. Jesus in two cases used the word to describe his own healing activity (Matt. 8.7 and Luke 14.3), but he also used it in the imperative when he commissioned the disciples for their ministry (Matt. 10.8, to the Twelve; Luke 10.9, to the Seventy). There is an immediacy about the word, both in the commissioning of the disciples and in the descriptions of Jesus's healing activity. So, except in two cases where the work of physicians is indicated, it does not in the Gospels convey the sense of ongoing treatment nor its original sense of continuous attendance and service. The sick whom Jesus treated underwent an immediate and complete cure, and this is the healing described by the word *therapeuō* in the Gospels.

The third word is *iaomai*, the noun *iatros* meaning a physician. Not surprisingly, perhaps, it is Luke the doctor who uses it most frequently. From earliest times *iaomai* was used in the medical sense of healing or curing, and in the Gospels is used almost exclusively of physical healing. Luke often replaces Matthew's *ther-*

apeuō with his preferred medical word *iaomai*, though he as frequently rings the changes between them (e.g. in 9. 1 and 2 he uses both words, for 'cure diseases' and 'heal' respectively). They are also used synonymously in the Fourth Gospel, and this seems to be the general verdict of the Gospel writers: there is not a great deal of difference between their meanings.

As we consider the essential meaning of Christian healing we shall find it helpful to recall the background meaning of these three words, which will all make a contribution to our understanding of the term. We may remind ourselves that there is a wholistic implication in the verb *sōzō*, in which lies the essential meaning of delivering and making the whole person safe from disease. And that is so, whether that disease is afflicting the physical or the spiritual part of the person, or both, for the different elements that constitute a person are totally interconnected and interwoven. Health and salvation, healing and saving find their logical connection in the words *sōtēria* and *sōzō*, for God is concerned for the total redemption of the whole person.

Therapeuō too has its contribution to make to the concept of Christian healing. The basic idea of service to, or attendance on, a person; the notion of willingness to serve, and of the need for a personal relationship between the attendant and the person being ministered to; these all combine further to elucidate the meaning of Christian healing. The Master who came among us 'as he who serves', who took a towel and washed the feet of his disciples, and who loved his own to the end, demonstrated in his own person the essential prerequisites for Christian healing. Such healing is above all costly, and the sum total paid by the Master who trained us and commissioned us in the ministry and service of Christian healing was the cross. This is not a service to be engaged in or entered upon lightly; neither can it be undertaken by anyone devoid of compassion and deep caring for the sufferer. The relationship has to be wrought in God, so that the sufferer experiences the presence and power of God communicated through the person giving the service. Essentially Christian healing is *Christ* healing.

Again, *iaomai* contributes to our understanding of Christian healing, for the healing that Christ wills for us is just as likely to come through the attendance of the professional practitioner, whether doctor, nurse or other medical worker. After all, they spend their whole lives 'anointing' people with the right medicaments, and in laying on of hands. It is good to be reminded that a doctor wrote one of the four Gospels (and how keenly he observed Jesus's healing ministry) as well as the first history book of the Church. It was natural for Luke to prefer this medical term for what he saw the disciples doing in Jesus's name, and he invested it with a fuller meaning, while still demonstating that the doctors' skills are given by God. We need also to be reminded that in our praying for the healing of the sick we should cover the whole medical team in attendance. Such prayer may well open the way for the healing Christ to work through the treatment they are offering.

Christian healing, then, is first and foremost about Christ. It follows the pattern he set in his own ministry, and the commission he gave to his disciples, and the fact that it happens at all is the fruit of his work, both in the creation and in the salvation of humankind. In both these mighty works humankind has been created, and recreated, in the image of God – has been made whole. This is what distinguishes Christian healing from other types of healing, such as spiritual healing (i.e. the curing of physical symptoms by spiritual means) or faith healing (i.e. the insistence on the patient's having sufficient faith to be healed before treatment is given). Of course a person's spirit and faith are often key elements in Christian healing, but Christian healing involves much more than that. It is the whole work of Christ in a person's body, mind and spirit, designed to bring that person to the wholeness which is God's will for us all.

Ultimately, as Christians, we cannot rightly separate health (i.e. the end product of the healing process) and salvation. We saw this when we looked at the most important word used in the New Testament to describe the work of Jesus Christ – *sōzō*. Both meanings are united in that word. When we talk of Christian healing, therefore, we mean the process towards the total salvation of the person. This will include the healing of the body and the mind, as well as the healing of the soul. Jesus Christ wants us whole in every dimension of our being.

I close this first chapter by quoting two Archbishops, first the former (Anglican) Archbishop of Canterbury, and secondly the present (Roman Catholic) Archbishop of Westminster. The words are those with which I described their views in *The Christian Healing Ministry*:[3]

Dr Coggan, who has done much to underline the healing dimension in the Church's witness, prefers to begin with the name Jesus. 'Here was an idea whose roots went deep down into Jewish soil. Jesus – Joshua – deliverance *from* and *to*. . . . The Name which is above every name is derived from a Hebrew root that denotes "to be spacious".' A Christian can never discuss healing without having Jesus in mind. His very name, the equivalent of Saviour from the root save/ heal, speaks of growth and enlargement, a process

6

whereby a power is unleashed that brings the life of man (or society) back into a new spaciousness in which all the cells (or members) are released and delivered to perform their full and purposeful function. Little wonder . . . that Jesus spent so much of his time in healing; it was part of his very nature to do so. As we proceed with this study in healing we must not forget this idea of spaciousness and growth. It goes back to the unleashing of the explosive force inherent in the act of creation, a power in nature that can even use suffering for an eventual good and takes setbacks into its evolutionary process.

Healing is as wide as creation and is the motive force within it. It must never be narrowed to a part of the whole. Too often we tend to think of physical healing only, but the purpose of our Creator for us is infinitely greater. He has unleashed a power that must heal totally and bring us into that spaciousness of health. Tyndale rightly translated *sōtēria* in this way at Luke 19.9, when Jesus declared on being received by Zacchaeus, 'Today *health* has come to this house.' Had we kept Tyndale's translation *health* and *heal* throughout the Bible instead of *salvation* and *save*, our ideas on the subject might have been more spacious![4]

And the second:

The initiative for the world's health lies with Christians. It is high time to wake out of sleep; our health is nearer now than when we first believed! Are we sufficiently concerned for the health of others? As Cardinal Basil Hume told his monks: 'The Gospel is not only a programme for action, it is also a proclamation of the power at our disposal. Forgiving and

7

healing should characterize our treatment of each other. Christ's manner of action has to be the model of ours. As pastors, we need to learn how to use his healing power, or how to be instruments enabling him to exercise that power on one another.'[5]

It seems to me that both make a contribution to our understanding of Christian healing.

2

IS HEALTH IMPORTANT
IN THE BIBLE?

The Bible lays emphasis on two important truths concerning the nature of mankind:

1. The first is that in essence human nature is fundamentally good, whatever 'foreign' elements may later have infiltrated our being. The author of Genesis (1.27 and 31) declares an important truth when he writes:

So God created man in his own image,
in the image of God he created him;
male and female he created them. . . .
God saw all that he had made, and it was very good.

In other words, there is in nature a tendency to heal. Cut down a tree and it tends to sprout up again; cut your finger and it tends to heal. It seems that healing is the Creator's will for us.

That healing is God's will for us has been proved by one of the most momentous discoveries of our generation – the DNA in every human being. It stands for Deoxyribonucleic acid, which scientists call 'the code of life'. The fascinating truth is that we received the DNA molecule in the first cell from our parents at our conception. (This discovery has surely undermined the pro-abortion cause.) It can only be viewed under an electron microscope, when tiny strands in the form of a spiral staircase, measuring six feet in some cases, can be discerned. Like recording tape it contains instructions and blueprints for more than a lifetime. It instructed our cells to separate, and so growth was made possible. It sends instructions to the brain to meet any emergency, which the brain with its 10 billion cells (neurons) and 500 trillion connections in its circuitry (synapses) – a computer more wonderful than any that could be invented by man – then puts into action. In computer language, *we are programmed for health*. One doctor has in fact said, 'The more closely I examine the human body, and the more I study its built-in ability to fight sickness and disease, I wonder how anyone gets sick.'[6] Science thus supports the theological insight of the Bible, that health and healing is the will of God for humankind.

2. The second truth the Bible puts forward is that human nature is an integral whole, and must be treated as such. We saw this in the use of the word *sōzō* in the New Testament. God wills the salvation/healing of the whole person. Indeed, Jesus Christ came as the Saviour/ Healer of the whole being of humankind, not just of a series of individuals, nor even the sum of their parts. He demonstrated this in his healing ministry: he always treated people wholistically, focusing unerringly on the root cause of their disease, whether it was unforgiven sin or an unhealed relationship.

George Bennett, the great pioneer in the healing ministry, used to point out how Jesus treated people as whole persons, ministering to them on three levels. The first level was that of the presenting illness or its symptoms. The second was what underlay those symptoms, what today we should call the environmental factors. These might be external to the person, e.g. the climate, or a stressful living situation; or internal, e.g. anxiety, resentment, jealousy, hatred. Every good doctor is aware of these two levels. The third was the spiritual level, at which patients might be under an evil influence, or obsessed with some fear from which they needed deliverance. Jesus was keen to ensure that people were healthy at all three of these levels, because he looked on sickness of any sort as an enemy invader, marring the perfection of his Father's Kingdom. Concern for people's health was one of Jesus's priorities, for this reason. His whole mission was after all centred on the proclamation of the Kingdom of God, a task he sought to accomplish by teaching, preaching and healing (Matt. 4.23; 9.35).

Jesus also accepted the Old Testament ideas on health, thinking as a Jew would – corporately – about the health of the individual only within the context of the health of the community and the nation. As the Old Testament writers saw it, life was not merely a matter of physiological function: it also involved moral activity and spiritual achievement. The quality of life was what mattered. Health is basically a state of wholeness and fulfilment of man's being, which was viewed as an undivided entity. Modern physicists might call it a totally interconnected system.

The word that comes nearest to expressing this idea of health is *shalom*, a word hard to translate into English which implies not only peace (the usual translation) but completeness, soundness, total well-being, wholeness, even prosperity. The World Health Organization came a long way towards this concept when it defined health as 'a state of complete physical, mental and social well-being and not merely the absence of disease and infirmity'. For the Jews, however, *shalom* was a gift from God, and human beings could find complete wholeness and their true fulfilment only in God.

Again, health in the Old Testament on its ethical side consisted in *obedience* to God's Law. Such obedience would bring health, while disobedience would lay one (or one's tribe) open to dis-ease. At the revelation of Jahweh to the Israelites at Marah as their Healer, we read 'If you listen carefully to the voice of the LORD your God and do what is right in his eyes, if you pay attention to his commands and keep all his decrees, I will not bring on you any of the diseases I brought on the Egyptians, for I am the LORD who heals you' (Exodus 15.26). We might also compare Leviticus 26.14–16 and Proverbs 3.7, 8. Health is more than freedom from disease, and so regular obedience to the Law was the Israelite's highway to wholeness and well-being. It would ensure a right relationship with God which was the foundation of health, the source of all blessing. Jesus finally pronounced the recipe for health in the Sermon on the Mount, particularly in the Beatitudes, one of which sums up in a positive fashion the benefits of obedience: 'Blessed are the pure in heart for they will see God' (Matt. 5.8).

There is also a third word we should note in the Old Testament, and that is *righteousness*, which covers the spiritual conception of health. The original idea behind this word in Hebrew and Aramaic was deliverance and salvation, which would be the fruit of a right relationship with God. So the word also contains the idea of straightness, conformity to a norm, and in the case of humankind, this norm is the character of God, in whose image we are made (Genesis 1.27).

This idea of having good relationships, which make an important contribution towards a person's health and well-being, is a factor common to all these three words expressing the idea of health in the Old Testament. One of our biblical scholars, the late Bishop Stephen Neill, went so far as to say there were four relationships that had to be in good order for a person to be healthy: the relationships with God, with one's neighbour, with one-self and with the soil. The first two form the subject of the two commandments of the Deuteronomic law, affirmed by Jesus. The third – with oneself – is too frequently neglected, although, like the Prodigal, we need to come to ourselves, to face our inner selves, if we are to be whole people. To achieve this many of us will need the help of a competent and experienced spiritual guide at some time in our life. The fourth relationship – with the soil – is one at which modern industrial and technological man has not excelled. Our pollution of the earth has led to much of our ill-health and dis-ease. All in all, we need to take very seriously what the Old Testament has to say about relationships, especially our relationship with God. Perhaps we would then realize how much teaching on health it contains.

I have written elsewhere[7] of Jesus's concern about healing and health. Suffice it to say here that he invariably showed compassion, and healed any sick who were brought to him. We never read of his turning anyone away. He gives the impression that his Father's will for us is health, and that sickness is a disfigurement of his Father's creation. He healed on the Sabbath, for instance, to show that a person's health and well-being was of greater consequence than a strict obedience to the law. A third of the content of the Gospels is about Jesus bringing men and women to health, in two cases about bringing them from the dead. He commissioned the disciples to heal the sick, and the Acts of the Apostles is a record of their obedience to that commission. The Bible lays constant emphasis on the well-being and health of humankind. There is plenty of reference to suffering, but mostly to suffering inflicted by others or incurred because of persecution, of which the cross is the prime

13

example, rather than because of sickness, which the New Testament teaches us should be eradicated from the face of the earth.

3

WHAT WAS ST PAUL'S
'THORN IN THE FLESH'?

Many books and learned articles have been written on this subject which has mystified scholars down the centuries. Not surprisingly it is still a matter of debate and interest, and is sometimes a stumbling-block for those trying to be more involved in Christ's healing ministry. The 'thorn in the flesh' was not necessarily a physical disease, though many commentators have concluded it to be so. Other suggestions have either been in the category of persecution or sexual desire. It may be as well to have the passage before us, from 2 Corinthians 12. 7–10:

> To keep me from becoming conceited because of these surpassingly great revelations, there was given me a thorn in my flesh, a messenger of Satan, to torment me. Three times I pleaded with the Lord to take it away from me. But he said to me, 'My grace is sufficient for you, for my power is made perfect in weakness.' Therefore I will boast all the more gladly about my weaknesses, so that Christ's power may rest on me. That is why, for Christ's sake, I delight in weaknesses, in insults, in hardships, in persecutions, in difficulties. For when I am weak, then I am strong.

St Paul calls the thorn 'a messenger of Satan'. A thrust from the shadow side could be in the form of opposition to his gospel, either from people, especially the Jews, or from a single, persistent person. Certainly the word 'messenger', which translates the Greek 'angel', is personal, and need not refer to sickness at all. Usually Christian preachers and leaders have at least one cross to bear in this respect, a person or persons who persistently oppose what they say or do. St Paul's uncompromising gospel would obviously provoke this kind of opposition, especially from his own countrymen, as his letters make plain. He took it, as many preachers have taken it since, as a hair shirt to prevent undue elation or pride.

So persistent was this messenger of Satan, however, that Paul pleaded three times with the Lord for its removal. His prayer was answered, though in the negative. The actual answer has proved to be a very great blessing, not only to the person to whom it was given, but to countless Christians ever since: 'My grace is sufficient for you, for my power is made perfect in weakness.'

The positive fruit of Paul's hardship is seen in this 'revelation'. The grace of God is indeed always sufficient for us if we will only turn to him as Paul obviously did, and place our total reliance on his sustaining strength. That ceaseless supply of God's grace is always sufficient for all our needs. And the second part of the revelation is also of very great significance, for it is only when we ourselves get out of the way with our selfishness and self-reliance, sometimes even with our over-weening kindness and well-meaning concern, that God can get *in* the way and show his power in us or in others for whom we have a care. There are times, more frequent than we imagine, when we have to 'let go and let God'. We are not to put ourselves in his place but at his feet. Paul shows us the way – 'I will boast all the more gladly about my weaknesses' – and only with this self-negating attitude, this Christ-like humility, will God's power have any place in us. Great Christian leaders seem to have needed this kind of reminder of their own weakness and so of God's greatness to fulfil a ministry of Christ-like power. Thomas à Becket, who wielded great power as Archbishop of Canterbury and dared to oppose his king (Henry II) and former friend, fighting for the rights of the Church against the State, was discovered by his grieving monks as they ministered to his truncated body after his murder in Canterbury Cathedral to be wearing under his blood-stained habit 'a covering of filthy sack-cloth and a horsehair shirt, long-worn and alive with lice. Beneath it they saw the festering weals of repeated self-scourging.'[8] The 'thorn' in Thomas's flesh was self-inflicted, while Paul's was 'given', but both were means of dealing with temptations to pride and power.

It seems therefore that, rather than a physical complaint, Paul's thorn in the flesh may have been more of a spiritual problem. Of course those who support the notion that it was a physical disease have used their ingenuity and come up with many and varied suggestions. The most frequent concerns some disease of the eyes, based on Paul's statement in Galatians 4.13–15. Epilepsy and migraine have also been suggested, and some think he had an impediment in his speech (see 2 Corinthians 10.1, 10; 11.6). The fact remains however that only someone with an exceptional constitution and blessed with good health could have undertaken the punishing schedule which Paul set himself and also survived the physical battering and suffering he endured 'for the sake of the gospel' (see 2 Corinthians 11.22–31).

My own view inclines to some spiritual trouble, possibly a susceptibility to depression, especially after being given the 'great revelations' referred to in the early part of 2 Corinthians 12. The spiritual life knows its high points but also its troughs, the dark nights of the soul. In point of fact depression is a debilitating illness, and we know that Paul prayed earnestly three times to be released from his trouble. To a preacher of the good news of Jesus Christ such an attack, especially before presenting the gospel for the first time before non-believers, would be a grievous disability, and would be seen as an assault from the shadow side sent to torment him and prevent the message getting across. But Paul learned through his prayer that such weakness could be the very source of real strength, as God was then able to take over the whole situation and to speak through this weakened vessel, this 'pot of earthenware'. In human weakness the grace of God could abound. Paul's thorn in the flesh not only taught the Apostle, but also has taught the Church down the ages, that the reason for which it was given – for the greater glory of God and the out-working of his grace – is in the end of far greater importance than the actual nature of this 'messenger of Satan'.

4

DID MIRACLES OF HEALING ONLY HAPPEN IN NEW TESTAMENT TIMES?

I am fortunate to have served in two Yorkshire parishes whose patron saints in their lifetime had active healing ministries. The people to whom they ministered would have answered this question with a resounding negative.

The first was St William of York, born at Weaverthorpe. There is a massive window in the north choir transept of York Minster depicting scenes from William's life. In many of them he is to be seen healing the sick or saving peoples' lives by his prayers, for example when the Ouse bridge collapsed as he was being welcomed back to York.

The other parish, St Martin-on-the-hill, Scarborough, had a patron who was not only a holy man and great Christian leader of the fourth century, but also had a powerful healing ministry. I am grateful to Dr Rex Gardner who has done valuable research[9] and, like me, believes that Martin's contemporary biographer, Sulpicius Severus, is to be relied upon. After meeting the saint Severus gave up his legal practice in order to examine the evidence of Martin's healing ministry critically, and to write his life.

'The gift of accomplishing cures,' declared the biographer, 'was so largely possessed by Martin that scarcely any sick persons came to him for assistance without being at once restored to health.' His methods were instructive. When he healed a paralysed girl, at the strong beseeching of her father, he put first things first: 'Betaking himself to his familiar arms in affairs of that kind, he cast himself down on the ground and prayed.' He then blessed the oil and poured it into the girl's mouth, and she recovered. (Appropriately enough, when the late Margaret Cropper wrote a pageant on the life of St Martin for our centenary, a surgeon took the part of Sulpicius Severus.) It is little wonder that Martin had such a tremendous influence on the growth of the Church at the time; his radiant and powerful faith affected all he met, St Ninian of Scotland being one. Within a few years of his death churches were being dedicated to him all over Christendom.

It seems that the light of Christ's healing power has not been totally extinguished during the intervening centuries. St Francis was also known for his healing ministry. Healings were associated with revival at the time of the Scottish Reformers and the Wesleys in the eighteenth century; and now we are witnessing new signs of it today. But let us go back for a moment and try to understand why, for a certain period, the idea that there was a cessation of healing after New Testament times gained ground.

In most generations Christians have looked back to apostolic times and marvelled at the 'many wonders and miraculous signs done by the apostles' (Acts 2.43). How were they to account for the paucity or perhaps non-existence of such signs in their own day? The easiest way – for it seemed logical and rational – was to say that such signs were part of the apostolic age, or as one writer put it, 'part of the credentials of the Apostles as the authoritative agents of God in founding the Church'.

The miraculous signs of healing, however, were only part of the Holy Spirit's gifts, and these gifts were given to the whole Church from the very first, not to specific individuals. As St Paul makes clear in 1 Corinthians 12, the gifts are part of the economy of the Church as the Body of Christ. Each one is necessary for the full functioning of the Body and all are complementary to each other. If this is true of the apostolic age of the Church it must be true of all ages. 'Jesus Christ is the same yesterday and today and for ever' (Hebrews 13.8), and so his Body the Church is not just for one generation but for all times until his coming again. St Paul was speaking through the Corinthians to all generations when he said, 'Now you are the body of Christ, and each one of you is a part of it. And in the church God has appointed first of all apostles, second prophets, third teachers, then workers of miracles, also those having gifts of healing, those able to help others, those with gifts of administration, and those speaking in different kinds of tongues.' (1 Cor. 12.27f.) All these are gifts given by God for the upbuilding of the Church through history. 'His touch has still its ancient power.' To believe that this power as it were dried up after the apostolic age is to make our God far too small. It is also to fly in the face of hard facts.

The Patristic writers all witnessed to the continuance of healing miracles in their day. In the second century Irenaeus wrote of Christians who 'still heal the sick by laying their hands upon them, and they are made whole'. He also said that it was impossible to number the gifts which the Church, scattered throughout the world, had received from God in the name of Jesus Christ. Tertullian, early in the third century, told how the Emperor Severus was healed by holy anointing at the hands of a Christian called Proculus. Dr Gardner comments that Severus died in Eboracum, our city of York, and if he were to return there today would find these same gifts being given by God and used to his glory, as I myself can testify, having had a share in the Christian community there.

It seems that in no generation has God left himself without witness in the matter of healing gifts, though in some eras of the Church such witness has been low-key, and God's gift to just a few members of the Body of his Son has kept the light aglow. Certainly in our own generation there is a remarkable revival of the spiritual gifts, helped on by a renewal of faith in the living God and a newness of life in the Churches not seen for many generations. There is also a new openness and better communication between the Churches. Indeed one is led to feel that if only the Churches themselves were healed together, the power of healing would flow mightily. The sin of schism, which we see rearing its ugly head yet again, diminishes the power and frustrates the purposes of God. From this we need wholesale repentance, that is, a turning round, back to God. A single-minded openness to Christ who prayed that we all might be one, an acknowledgment of our total dependence on him, and an utter devotion to God who alone gives these gifts to his Church in the power of the Spirit, has always been the foundation charter of the Church, which needs such largesse of spirituality to perform its task in each generation. Meanwhile, the Lord of the Church does not withdraw his blessings, and there are many signs and wonders that betoken his presence in our time.

John Wimber, whose ministry, marked out by such signs and wonders, has helped and greatly influenced many people, is also an accomplished teacher, and has defined this type of ministry as follows:[10]

By power evangelism I mean a presentation of the gospel that is rational but also transcends the rational. The explanation of the gospel comes with a demonstration of God's power through signs and wonders. Power evangelism is a spontaneous, Spirit-inspired, empowered presentation of the gospel. Power evangelism is that evangelism which is preceded and undergirded by supernatural demonstrations of God's presence.

Through these supernatural encounters people experience the presence and power of God. Usually this occurs in words of knowledge, healing, prophecy, and deliverance from evil spirits. In power evangelism, resistance to the gospel is supernaturally overcome, and receptivity to Christ's claims is usually very high.

Wimber goes on to point out that this was of course the essential ministry in New Testament times, when signs and wonders accompanied the apostles' preaching. And why? Because the apostles were obedient to Jesus' commission to preach the gospel and heal the sick. They were also high on expectation, which the rationalism of our contemporary world has diminished. In New Testament times preaching and healing together constituted the proclamation of the gospel (i.e. evangelism). This was the methodology of the early followers of Christ; they would never have considered doing anything else.

As I have already hinted, this is very hard for us to accept, given our current world-view. For the last two hundred years or so we in the West have been totally secular in our thinking and education, that is, our thinking has been within a frame of reference bounded by the limits of our life on earth. We have little or no place for the supernatural; our thought-systems seem to assume that we live in a universe shut off from divine intervention. Mercifully, as I have said elsewhere, the physicists are leading us back to a world-view that is more open to the supernatural by showing us how the various aspects of creation are interrelated and interconnected. In the future we may be more open to the occurrence of signs and wonders, as a result of this new world-view that is emerging. The fact is that they are happening in many of the revivalist Churches of our time, and indeed in the traditional Churches also, as we become more open to the power of the Holy Spirit.

If anyone seeks confirmation of our need to be open to the power of the Spirit, let him compare carefully his own Church's life and witness with that of the early Church described in Acts; and let him also look out on the world with its very great needs and see humankind's inability to meet them. 'Only those who hope in the Lord shall renew their strength' (Isaiah 40.31), and that means constant, ceaseless prayer, a renewal of the whole spiritual life of the Church and of each of its members. Our Lady of Medjugorje is asking this of Christians in our time. 'Pray, pray, pray' is her constant counsel. If we would accept her summons to prayer, signs and wonders would follow. And to those who see John Wimber as a gadfly to the Church of our time, I would only suggest that they consider how necessary is such a stimulus to each generation.

5

DOES GOD SEND AND
USE SUFFERING?

When people ask this question, they usually mean 'Does God send sickness and disease?' In reality, as we see from the New Testament, there is a distinction to be made between suffering and sickness. Sickness can of course involve suffering, both physical and mental, and possibly spiritual too. But if we turn to the New Testament the uniqueness of suffering will become apparent.

In St Mark's Gospel, Jesus reiterates a prophetic phrase three times: 'The Son of Man must suffer' (8.31; 9.31; 10.33). He did not say of himself that he must endure sickness or become the victim of some disease. On the contrary, it is noticeable that sickness and disease are never connected with the person of Jesus, who seems to have remained remarkably fit during his ministry, able to cope with long vigils of prayer alongside exceptionally busy periods of ministry from which the stress of opposition was rarely absent. Perhaps he was able to cope because of his long vigils of prayer. In any case the Evangelists never reported him as ailing from any sickness.

So what did Jesus mean, when he said 'The Son of Man must suffer'? His study of the Old Testament prophets had led him to the certain belief that as the Servant of the Lord he would have to suffer before his eventual triumph over the powers of darkness. In all probability, from the moment he accepted the role of the Servant-Messiah at his baptism, he knew that he must suffer death. Further research into the Old Testament would have convinced him that before the Son of Man could be glorified, he must first suffer many things (humiliating persecution), and be rejected by his generation. The idea of suffering was an essential ingredient in Jesus's conception of the Son of Man, and undoubtedly he saw this also as the lot of those who would follow him. The very language that he used – 'If anyone would come after me, he must take up his cross daily' – was sufficient indication of the cost of discipleship.

'Suffering' in the New Testament therefore means this cost of discipleship, and the inevitable persecution that a true follower of 'the Way' may have to face, rather than sickness and disease. But although a servant of God may have to face this kind of suffering, in persecution and in martyrdom, as we have constantly seen in our own generation, God does not *send* this or inflict it on his servants. We ourselves, through the evil that is in us, compounded of jealousy and anger, lust for power and innate violence, inflict such suffering on our fellow human beings. We should not blame God for this type of suffering.

Of course there is also suffering in sickness, and we must not dodge the question, 'Does God send sickness?' The Old Testament view, on the whole, was that he did. The infliction of the plagues on Egypt at a key time in Israelite history was to serve as a lasting reminder of God's displeasure, and this view persisted throughout the nation's history, especially with regard to leprosy. The uncleanness of that disease was seen as having a moral significance. And despite the positive healing ministry of Jesus, this view of sickness as a sign of God's displeasure persisted in the Christian Church, especially among the Reformers. In England, at any rate, successive English Prayer Books proclaimed the doctrine that sickness is a visitation from God: 'Whatsoever your sickness is, know you certainly, that it is God's visitation,' and 'Take, therefore, in good part the chastisement of the Lord'.

Jesus, on the other hand, when the disciples questioned him about this traditional Old Testament doctrine in relation to the man born blind, refuted the idea that it was sent by God because of the man's sins or because of the sins of his parents. Rather the reverse: 'This happened so that the work of God might be displayed in his life' (John 9.3). In other words, the work of God was to heal, as Jesus demonstrated by proceeding to heal the man's blindness.

One of the hardest tasks, therefore, that Christians called to serve in the ministry of the healing Christ face today, is to clear away and dispose of the hampering burden so many sick people bring to their situation – the belief, perhaps not articulate but held deep in their subconscious mind, that God has sent them the sickness as a punishment. Such a belief is a barrier to health, for it negates the healing power of Christ and separates the sick person from him who is the source of healing. Often the first task of the Christian minister is to reconcile the sick person with God, and sometimes even to heal the person's ideas of God. God is love; he loves his own to the uttermost, as Jesus showed by dying for us on the cross. By this act of redeeming love, as foretold in one of the Servant Songs,

> Surely he took up our infirmities
> and carried our sorrows. . .
> He was pierced for our transgressions. . .
> and by his wounds we are healed. (Isa. 53.4f)

Rather than sending us our sicknesses, God heals them

and takes them away. Jesus demonstrated this constantly in his healing ministry, as well as by the 'Exodus' of the New Testament, the cross/resurrection which unleashed the healing power enabling the disciples to carry out the Lord's commission to heal as well as preach. Wherever the good news is proclaimed in this way today, sicknesses and diseases will be healed – to God's glory. He is the author of healing rather than of sickness.

The question as to whether God, if he does not send sickness, uses it, must receive a decisive answer in the affirmative. Yes, of course he does. Most of us will have experience of this, either from personal knowledge, or from cases in which we have been involved. At its simplest, how often being put to bed with a common cold has saved a person from exhaustion, or even from some form of heart disease. Illness can take people out of situations of unbearable tension or responsibility, and during convalescence they may well come to a new view of their life and work. For many, hospitalization may be the first opportunity they have been given to sit back and ponder, at least as the painful symptoms disappear, on what their life is all about. If there is a sensitive medical staff member or chaplain available, or a Christian Listener, people can be brought to a healing much deeper than the cure of their sickness. God can really use that situation as people are led to ask themselves deeply spiritual questions – Why did this illness come? Why at this time? What if I had died? What shall I now do with the rest of my life? With sensitive leading, the sick can be helped to a profound Christian faith which will be a true healing and a major blessing for the rest of their lives.

Have you ever heard anyone say, 'Thank God I got cancer'? The reason is usually that the disease was cured, and the person led to a living faith in the living

Christ. The Acorn video[11] records the testimony of Anne White, a probation officer, who was healed from multiple sclerosis. At the end of her testimony she says that if she had to choose between her old life and the new, she would rather have multiple sclerosis back and keep her new-found Lord and Saviour, Jesus Christ. God mightily used her illness, not only to heal it, but to make her a strong witness for the Kingdom. And just as God can use our illness, so also, when we are well he can use our health, if we will only pause for a while to ponder some of these deeper questions in life. Being healed is a Damascus gate experience: it involves our life being turned around.

WHY ARE SOME PEOPLE HEALED AND OTHERS NOT?

There is no easy answer to this question, certainly not to the second part of it. As regards the first part, I have the overpowering conviction that the majority of those who experience some form of miraculous healing are healed for a purpose. It is as if God said to them, 'I want you alive on earth a little longer to fulfil my purposes of love, before I enfold you in my eternal love where all pain is taken away. For this purpose I heal you now'.

The experience I recall most vividly, which I have related elsewhere,[12] was of our verger in Scarborough, who was desperately ill in hospital. The surgeon kindly rang me up late on a Sunday night to warn me that our friend might not survive until the morning. Anne and I left at once for the hospital, as usual taking the oils. It was hard to get near him – in an oxygen tent and with drip feeds. I asked the nurse to draw the curtains round the bed – it was now very late, and others in the ward were attempting to get some sleep. She stayed with us as part of the Church at prayer. We noticed that he was barely conscious at the beginning, but that by the short thanksgiving after the anointing, he was able to join in the Lord's Prayer. He gripped our hands as we said 'good-night'.

When the nurse drew back the curtains, some of the men in the beds opposite were sitting up, wide awake. One of them called me over and silenced my attempted apology for disturbing him. In his straight Yorkshire manner he told me, 'Summat's 'appened be'ind them curtains'. He had picked up in his inner consciousness that the Lord was about his work and therefore all would be well. It was a prophetic remark, and I have often thought since then what sensitivity can lie behind a gruff exterior, and how this dear man rather showed up one of the Lord's priests as a man of little faith. I had been trying to confine the grace of the healing Christ behind curtains in case he disturbed anyone! At least I learned a great deal from that Yorkshireman, whom I shall always remember as the prophet of that memorable night.

In the morning, the day sister coming on duty remarked that the language in the ward had been cleaned up overnight! The doctors were puzzled that the patient's blood-count was normal. Within a fortnight he was back in church to a great welcome by a truly thankful congregation. He died two years later from the same disease, but it seemed to us that the Lord gave him those two years *of grace* in which to witness 'what great things *he* has done'. It was a seaside church, to which thousands of holiday-makers came in the season, and during those 'extra' two years he witnessed to countless numbers of them as well as to members of the regular congregation. He did much to encourage and enliven the faith of many individuals, but perhaps the greatest blessing of his healing was to the local church as the Body of Christ: it was a corporate blessing. We had been asking what the next step should be concerning the ministry of healing, having spent over five years as a prayer fellowship, undergirding God's work among the sick. Our verger's healing was a catalyst: we now knew where we had to go and what we had to do. 'Go, tell. . . .' It was a formative moment in the life of that congregation – and of its priest – and who can tell now to what his healing has led! There was a corporate purpose for his Church in what the Lord did that night, as well as an encouragement to the faith of so many individuals. How exciting it is to see the Lord at work and to ponder his purposes!

One of the most famous 'healings-with-a-purpose' (though I believe that all healings fulfil the purposes of God and are given for some reason) is that of Dorothy Kerin. Healed on 18 February 1912, this remarkable person was given fifty years of ministry and witness to the Lord's healing power. She had been seriously ill since her father's death in 1902, and on more than one occasion the doctor thought it little short of a miracle that she herself escaped death. She was extremely delicate. Diphtheria was followed by pneumonia and pleurisy. Her life was despaired of, but much prayer was offered – and answered. Her partial recovery followed 'immediately after receiving the Blessed Sacrament'. Eventually her illness was diagnosed as phthisis, and further suffering involved severe haemorrhage from the lungs and internal complications. She was taken home – to die. For three more years she was nursed by her mother. The doctors regarded her condition as hopeless, and for the last fortnight of her illness she was unconscious and blind. It was during those last two weeks that she later said the Lord had showed her spiritual realities. In that hinterland between life and death she had the out-of-body experience, but more than that, she was also given an experience of the life of the world to come. Finally, 'as I looked I saw One coming towards me, I thought he was coming for me, and held out my hand towards him, but he smiled and said, "No, Dorothy, you are not coming yet." Then a great light and a voice – "Dorothy, your sufferings are over. Get up and walk." '

When she opened her eyes, she was sitting up in bed surrounded by her family who had been summoned to say their farewells to the supposedly dying girl. She asked for her dressing-gown, telling them she was quite well now and must get up and walk. She was always instantly obedient to a divine prompting. Her mother and the others were however too astonished to answer her or to move. Again the voice – 'Get up and walk' – and she got out of bed unaided. She then went down two flights of stairs to the larder and brought back a trayful of food for 'a real meal'! Extensive examination by several doctors showed that her health had been completely restored. Fifty years later, after an inspired ministry of healing at home and abroad, she saw her church of Christ the Healer dedicated by Bishop Cuthbert Bardsley at Burrswood, the home of healing near Tunbridge Wells, where the Church and the medical profession work together in equal partnership. The more one ponders on the amazing life of this special person whom the Lord undoubtedly blessed, the more one is led to see a very definite purpose in her healing.[13]

So Yes, I do believe there is a reason why people are healed. In some tiny way it contributes to the divine ordering of things, since each one seems to be given a particular mission or purpose to fulfil for the remainder of their life on earth.

To answer the second part of the question – Why are some people *not* healed? – is more difficult. Ultimately the reason is known only to God, and therefore we cannot begin to know. That is not just ducking the question, it is the plain truth. However, sometimes it is possible to discern blockages to a person's healing *on a human level*. There are some people, surprising as it may seem, who do not really want to get well, possibly because they feel they could not face the demands made on a healthy person. Did Jesus detect this in the man at the Pool of Bethesda, who, like many, allowed circumstances to dominate his life (John 5.6)? It was like being in prison. Could he cope with life outside? He was used to being ill. There are many who may feel like that today, and it is a barrier to their healing.

Sin is another barrier which needs clearing out of the way. Jesus told the man at Bethesda, 'Stop sinning or something worse may happen to you' (John 5.14). Psychosomatic medicine has taught us that some burdens on the mind, such as unforgiven sin or a lack of forgiveness towards others, can cause a blockage in the body's immune system and healing capacities which prevents a return to health. The prayer that Jesus gave us is a good daily prescription, 'Forgive us our sins, for we also forgive everyone who sins against us' (Luke 11.4). Notice that he makes our forgiveness dependent on our forgiveness of others. James in his letter (5.16) exhorts his readers, 'Confess your sins to each other and pray for each other so that you may be healed'. In the Anglican Book of Common Prayer, the priest in exhorting people to prepare for Holy Communion says further, 'If there be any of you, who by this means cannot quiet his own conscience herein, but requireth further comfort or counsel, let him come to me, or to some other discreet and learned Minister of God's Word, and open his grief; that by the ministry of God's holy Word, he may receive the benefit of absolution . . . to the quieting of his conscience'. The Church is in the business of dealing with sin because its Lord and Master has once and for all dealt with the problem on the cross.

Bad relationships can also be a blockage to health, especially when there is a sourness between close members of a family. Such sourness leads to an unhealthy household. It seems as though a negative 'field' is emit-

34

ted which can be conducive to ill-health. We need to examine ourselves about that four-fold need for good relationships with God, with our neighbour (that is, with everyone we meet), with ourselves and with creation. As Bishop Stephen Neill said, if we have positive relationships with all four, we are on the road to health.

There are many reasons such as these on the human level why healing may not come. I would only add one more: lack of trust. Most of us would agree that if we do not trust our doctor, we are not likely to progress far on the road to health. I say *trust*, because even when we believe he is a very competent doctor with all the right qualifications, we also have to put our life in his hands, and that means trusting him. This is of course the sort of trust we express in the Christian creeds: not just saying we believe that God exists and sent his Son to earth two thousand years ago, but declaring our belief *in* Him, and our readiness to trust in him for the rest of our lives. This kind of belief in or trust involves total commitment. If we would become a whole person, with our relationships made healthy and our sins forgiven, with a new purpose to living and a new joy in life, then let us pray earnestly to God who heals and entrust our lives to him. Too many of us flirt with Christianity: we need to see it as a marriage, a commitment for life.

7

HOW CAN I FIND
INNER HEALING?

As long ago as 380 BC, Plato rebuked the medical profession of his day for separating soul from body and for daring to treat the one without the other. It is a sign of health today that forces are at work, in both Medicine and the Church, which stress the unity of the person and so offer treatment that is truly wholistic. After all, Jesus treated people wholistically, and Hippocrates laid down a code for treating people in the same way.

Today we can also accept the fact that men and women only find wholeness, even their very individuality, within the network of human relationships, in a word – within community. We have taken some time to come round to this way of thinking because we went down the avenue of Greek, individualistic, thought, rather than the Hebrew way of corporate thinking in terms of the community.

The Bible is essentially the book of a community. The Old Testament records the history of the chosen community of Israel. We find it difficult to know whether writers refer to the man or the tribe, when 'Israel' is mentioned. This idea of corporate personality led to the belief that one person's sins would bring disaster on the whole family, just as a blessing for one was a blessing for all. So health and disease were thought of in corporate terms – as affecting the whole community. For instance, in the case of the 'suffering servant' of Isaiah, the bearing of stripes by one man led to a corporate healing of all.

This corporate dimension was accepted by Jesus, who called himself the representative 'Son of man.' He becomes the suffering servant, and identifies himself with suffering humanity. His victory over sin and death is theirs, and every follower to the end of time is *incorporated* in his Body through dying and rising again with him in baptism. The New Testament is full of organic models which describe this corporateness – the vine, the body, the bride, the building. So the corporate truth unfolds, 'As in Adam all die, so in Christ all will be made alive' (1 Cor. 15.22). Here alone, in the corporate solidarity of being together in Christ, is health and wholeness, healing and eternal life, sonship and salvation. This corporateness has immense implications for our health and healing.

Today we are coming to see that health is often determined by relationships. This is in fact nothing new. The Deuteronomic code insisted on a good relationship with God and with one's neighbour as a basis of living. These were relationships that had to be worked at and required a total commitment: 'Love the Lord your God with all your heart and with all your soul and with all your strength. These commandments that I give you today are to be upon your hearts. Impress them on your children. Talk about them when you sit at home and when you walk along the road, when you lie down and when you get up' (Deuteronomy 6. 5–7). The commandments, which dealt entirely with these two relationships, with God and neighbour, were meant to fill the inner consciousness of both the individual and the nation. 'Attention to these laws' even brings an assurance of health: 'The Lord will keep you free from every disease' (Deuteronomy 7. 12,15).

Research has shown in our time that a lack of quality

in these essential relationships can combine with other material factors to produce a group pathology. Such emotions as fear, anxiety, indifference, or selfishness occurring within a group or household can affect the health of the group. It can affect individual health too, of course: envy or hatred or malice, for instance, can actually change the structure of the lining of a person's stomach. The body and the mind influence each other both corporately and individually.

There is then, in both theology and medicine, a new emphasis on the way in which a person's health and individual salvation are wrapped up in the community. This concept is essentially biblical, so it is a *re*discovery. We must beware, therefore, of thinking that healing, even inner healing, is just a personal, individual matter between each of us and our Maker.

This is borne out by the story of a girl who was grievously sick and, at death's door, read her Bible and learned from James 5.14–16 that she must call for the Elders of her Church. When they came they did not know what to do, but after a long silence one confessed his sins, then another, and another, until all the grudges and acts of jealousy between them came out. Then the girl confessed her sins. Finally they all prayed for forgiveness – and the girl got better. The girl was through her clinical condition bearing the guilt of her congregation. Only Jesus Christ, the head of the Body, could heal at that depth.

Perhaps the greatest need for our health today, especially as a community and as a nation, is the inner healing that would free us to live life to the full, and so grow together 'unto the measure of the stature of the fullness of Christ'. How shall we attempt this?

I would suggest that the most beneficial context for

such inner healing is the context of praise. C.S. Lewis once said that 'praise is inner health made audible'. And of course the supreme act of the Church's praise is the Eucharist – *the* Thanksgiving. Here is the time when the Body meets together and so the corporateness of the healing is preserved. When we pray for inner healing we are praying for a grateful, a eucharistic, memory. And the Eucharist is the grateful memory of the Church, when we 'proclaim the Lord's death until he comes' (1 Corinthians 11.26), when we *re*live, *re*call the salvific event of the death and resurrection of Jesus Christ, and 'give thanks to him for his great glory'.

So too we should be able to recall our whole life, our own experiences, great and small, joyful and painful, from yesterday or the remote past, and to praise God for them. If we are not able to praise God for some event in our past life, it may well be a sign that we need inner healing for that hurt.

When Ruth Carter Stapleton came to York at the time when her brother was President of the United States, I had the privilege of chairing her meeting, which was of course packed out, and was able to observe her closely. She had to leave in one hour in order to catch her plane back to London (which she herself paid for). She stood motionless, but spoke with utter conviction, prayerful to a degree, completely serene, and seemingly oblivious of time for she never looked at a clock or watch. She finished after fifty-nine minutes, we bowed our heads in prayer, and she left.

She told a story about herself, of a time when she felt down and depressed, and wondered if it was due to any sin or bitterness in her life. As she went to sleep that night she prayed that God would reveal the source of her problem. When she awoke she remembered an incident from her childhood. As a young girl she had returned home from school one day to find her elder sister in the kitchen making a magnificent sandwich. How she wanted that sandwich! So when her sister was putting things away, she grabbed it and ran. But her sister had longer legs and was catching up with her, so Ruth decided that if she could not have the sandwich, no-one would, and threw it in the incinerator.

She immediately telephoned her sister and asked if she remembered the incident. She did, and then Ruth confessed her shame and asked her sister's forgiveness. After freely giving it her sister said, 'I'm glad that is now cleared away because I have never felt at one with you or loved you as I should since that time'. Ruth could not praise God for that event when she remembered it, and so she had to confess it, and that led to a healing with her sister. In her book *The gift of inner healing* she reminded us of how computer scientists coined the word 'GIGO', meaning 'Garbage in, garbage out'. So if garbage has been fed into our subconscious, garbage is going to emerge. We shall need a spring clean, but then need to be filled in every part with praise – with the love of the Holy Name and with the grace and power of the Holy Spirit. Ruth also said: 'Inner healing is a ladder, not a single rung'; a process, rarely a one-time event.

Sometimes in prayer, and perhaps especially at the Eucharist as we *re*call the past corporately as part of the Body of Christ, we shall be made aware of some hurt or sin that needs forgiveness and healing. Frequently we shall be able to deal with this ourselves there and then. We acknowledge the wound, bring it to Jesus, perhaps at the offertory or when we come to the Communion rail, and *surrender it to him*. We ask him to come into that part of our life and heal the memory, and visualize him bringing peace and harmony to any hurtful scene. Then we ask him to make us grateful, part again of his eucharistic community.

So 'Forget it' is bad advice when people have been hurt. That means the memory is suppressed – the garbage remaining inside. The hurt has to surface in the end if we would be healed. Even eminent professional people, great leaders, can have their well-being undermined by suppressed memories. If they are in positions of responsibility then of course the dis-ease can affect the lives of others through their unhealed attitudes and one-sided judgements. And often an unhealed memory is the cause of sadness or depression in someone's life.

Only Jesus Christ can heal at this level. The essential need is to bring the dis-ease straight to Christ in the Eucharist and ask him to deal with it, there and then, when the Body is assembled in the act of recalling him and his redemptive activity. As Robert Faricy has said: 'The eucharist applies the healing power of the Cross of Jesus.'[14] The cross is the source of this corporate healing: 'But I, when I am lifted up from the earth, will draw all men to myself' (John 12.32). The crucified Christ is the focal point of God's healing power for the human race. He is the Saviour and Healer of all, and the cross is the place where all may find healing. And after his cross and resurrection, Jesus demonstrated that healing power in the threefold recalling of Peter (John 21.15ff). It seems as if Jesus takes Peter through a healing of the memories of that black night of his betrayal, made all the more poignant by the three questions corresponding to the three-fold denial, and brings him out into the clear light of a new dawn in his relationship both to Jesus himself and to humankind, commissioning him for his task as pastor of the Church and obviously supplying the grace that alone will make him sufficient for it.

Although this healing of Peter had corporate implications, as Jesus showed in the charge he gave him, it was a very individual case, which required the healing of the one-to-one relationship. Often this is our need also. We may find we are unable to deal with this sort of problem ourselves. We shall need a 'soul-friend', someone who can allow us to off-load, and give us wise counsel. We may also need a priest, who can give us 'the benefit of Absolution' and spiritual counsel. We may need longer counselling before some deep-seated hurts are removed. Sometimes we have to forgive ourselves before we can receive the healing blessings of God's forgiveness in its fulness. But of all the remedies, the healing grace of the Lord Jesus Christ is the sum. Only he can heal at the deepest levels of our consciousness and will – if we allow him to do so.

Since he is present 'in his timeless potency' (Bishop Michael Ramsey's phrase) at the Eucharist, when we 'proclaim the Lord's death until he comes' (1 Corinthians 11.26), inner healing can powerfully be received in the context of the Church's liturgy, all the more powerful for its being a corporate experience. This does, however, need a well-instructed congregation, and because in recent years we have made the Parish Eucharist 'the way in' to the Body of Christ, such a congregation is not always at hand. It is also essential for the congregation itself to be on the way towards being healed, with all animosities and resentments, jealousies and hurts, confessed and unloaded, so that the Holy Spirit can have free course among all its members and distribute the healing gifts as he determines (1 Corinthians 12. 7–11). The relevant teaching is found in the Sermon on the Mount:

If you are offering your gift at the altar and there remember that your brother has something against you, leave the gift there in front of the altar. First go and be reconciled to your brother; then come and offer your gift. (Matthew 5.23f)

We shall also find it helpful to observe a fast before Communion (see Matthew 6. 16–18), at least the traditional fast from midnight, so that there is a corporate preparation of the congregation. A 'like-mindedness' (see Philippians 2.1f) is needed in the Body of Christ, if it is to become a healed instrument, able to be a ministrant of healing to all who come within its embrace. Conflict may be fashionable today, but the way of conflict will not enable the Church of Christ to be an instrument of the Kingdom. We shall meet conflict enough in the world if we try to serve the Kingdom, but the weapon God can use to promote his purposes is a healed and united Church. Unhealed situations (and individuals) in the Body are detrimental to the calling of the Church, and can best be dealt with when its members are gathered together to recall Christ into the midst. The Eucharist is 'a sacrament of love, a sign of unity, a bond of charity' (Constitution on the Sacred Liturgy, No. 47). Father Jim McManus CSSR shows how the Eucharist is such a healing liturgy.[15] We begin by confessing our sins and receiving 'the benefit of Absolution'. In the Kyries it is as if we say, 'You were sent to heal the contrite, Lord have mercy'. 'Lord Jesus, you heal the wounds of sin and division, Christ have mercy.' As the ministry of the word develops, having been made aware of our sinfulness at the beginning, we increasingly experience the healing purposes and mercies of the ever-present Lord, culminating in the act of Communion before which we say,

'Lord, I am not worthy to receive you, but only say the word and I shall be healed.'

The Church has in fact always prayed for the healing of the whole person just before Communion. In the priest's prayer before receiving he asks 'Lord Jesus Christ, with faith in your love and mercy I eat your body and drink your blood. Let it not bring me condemnation but *your healing of my mind and body*.' Also, in a prayer usually said silently after the *Our Father*, he prays,

> Deliver us, Lord, from every evil,
> and grant us peace in our day.
> In your mercy keep us free from sin
> and protect us from all anxiety.

Here again Jesus's teaching in the Sermon on the Mount (Matt. 6.25–34) points to the importance of this prayer against anxiety at this key point in the Liturgy. Freedom from anxiety is a healthy condition to be sought after with all our might, as Jesus underlined in his teaching. Father McManus quotes a psychiatrist as saying that about ninety per cent of his patients were mentally sick because of anxiety, and that anxiety is a spiritual condition which he could do very little to alleviate. The answer to anxiety is trust in God, and the Eucharist is the healing-ground for such dis-ease, because there Christ is present to the whole Body, permeating and re-creating the very being of every member with himself and all his healing potency. Appropriately, Dr Kenneth McAll refers to this 'treatment' as a Eucharist of Resurrection.[16]

I have tried to show how each of us may seek and find (see Matthew 7.7) inner healing, and I have concentrated on the Eucharist, when Christ is present to the whole Body. I end with two quotations, the first a prayer

44

from the Good Friday Liturgy, frequently said as a Thanksgiving for the Eucharist or after Absolution:

Almighty and eternal God,
you have restored us to life
by the triumphant death and resurrection of Christ.
Continue this healing work within us.
May we who participate in this mystery
never cease to serve you,

and we might add:

through his healing name of Jesus. Amen.

The second is from the much-loved Psalm 103.1–5, 22:

Praise the Lord, O my soul;
all my inmost being, praise his holy name.
Praise the Lord, O my soul,
and forget not all his benefits.

He forgives all my sins
and heals all my diseases;
he redeems my life from the pit
and crowns me with love and compassion.
He satisfies my desires with good things,
so that my youth is renewed like the eagle's. . . .

Praise the Lord, all his works
everywhere in his dominion.

Praise the Lord, O my soul.

May we make these prayers our own.

8

DO CERTAIN PEOPLE HAVE A GIFT OF HEALING, AND HOW DO I KNOW IF I HAVE A GIFT?

When St Paul talked about gifts of healing in 1 Corinthians 12 – and he always used the plural, *gifts* – he did so in the context of teaching about the body of Christ, the Church. As always he taught thoroughly and made several important points:

1. *The Holy Spirit is given to enable men and women to confess the true faith, that 'Jesus is Lord' (v.3).* This was probably the original creed professed by a catechumen immediately prior to his baptism. It was said, so St Paul believed, under the inspiration of the Holy Spirit, because it was the greatest commitment a person could make. Jesus who was crucified and raised from the dead is professed to be the Lord of the Universe, of the Church and of the person making the confession. This is the Spirit's greatest gift, enabling a person to acknowledge and confess complete trust in the holy name of Jesus.

There is also transforming power in the name of Jesus, which means 'Saviour and Healer'. At the heart of Eastern Orthodox spirituality is the Jesus prayer, 'Lord Jesus Christ, Son of God, have mercy on me a sinner.' Believers are taught to say this constantly 'with the mind in the heart', so that the holy name becomes the central and focal point of their existence, so that Jesus's healing and saving grace may work in the inner recesses of their being and transform each of them into a Christ-likeness. Is there any greater gift that could be given at the instigation of the Spirit?

2. *God is the giver of all good gifts*: 'There are different kinds of gifts, but the same Spirit. There are different kinds of service' (*diakonia*, from which we get our word 'deacon'), 'but the same Lord. There are different kinds of working' (*energēmata*, from which comes the word 'energy'), 'but the same God works all of them in all people' (vv. 4–6). The Triune God, Father, Son and Holy Spirit, is the source of all these gifts, these ministries, these energies. There can be no ministry of healing, no gifts, no energies unless the glory is given totally to the God who gives. We recall the revelation at the waters of Marah, 'I am the Lord who heals you' (Exod. 15.26).

3. *These gifts of the Spirit are 'given for the common good'*(v. 7). They are not given for private aggrandisement or to create a cult surrounding a gifted individual. The exaltation of the ego in ministry is a dangerous phenomenon which always distorts the truth and distances us from the power of God, because he will not work where selfish motives creep in. God gives his gifts for the service of all humankind, to hasten his Kingdom and bring his creatures a new wholeness. They can never, must never, be kept for selfish gain, but must always be used for their inbuilt purpose, the good of the whole – Body, Church, world.

4. *The gifts of the Spirit are given to individual members only as the Holy Spirit wills*, and in each and every case gifts are given only through or by means of the Spirit. In the first list (vv. 8–10), 'gifts of healing' are itemized and so are 'miraculous powers'. We have already noted that St Paul uses the plural 'gifts', and deliberately. There are indeed many variations of the healing gifts, because of the great diversity of diseases

and human ailments. These gifts will vary considerably according to the will of the Holy Spirit by whose economy the Church is equipped to meet every occasion and every kind of ill. These gifts, which may be empathy or compassion, or a gift of intercession or diagnosis, or touch or counselling, or performing the practical tasks in a sick household – the list is endless – are mercifully totally under the Spirit's direction, who alone knows the needs of the Body of Christ and of the world to which it ministers. They are distributed at his will alone.

We may also note the words St Paul uses to describe the gifts in these instances. The 'gifts of healing' are *charismata iamatōn*. If the Church is truly Spirit-filled it is *charismatic* in the pure sense of being endowed with the gifts of the Spirit, without which it is unable to carry out the commission of Christ to proclaim the good news by preaching and healing. The word used for healing in this instance was originally a medical term, and as we would expect, is used mostly by St Luke, the doctor. 'Miraculous powers' is a translation of *energēmata dunameōn*, the words literally meaning 'energies of powers'. Both words are used in the Gospels in reference to Jesus's healing miracles. The Body of Christ is now the expression of the ministry of Jesus empowered by the Holy Spirit, who distributes the gifts as he wills.

5. *The Spirit has made us members of the Body of Christ, and it is only because of our membership that we receive his gifts.* 'We were all baptized by one Spirit into one body' (v. 13) says St Paul. Here is the context in which we become open to the Spirit and his gifts, a context in which no-one is special and yet all are special. No-one is continually given all the gifts while others are given none. The Body of Christ is the only fellowship in which all members – of all colours and races, sexes and

ages – are loved equally by 'the God and Father of our Lord Jesus Christ', who demonstrated the all-embracing love of the Father by his death on the cross. Truly it is the 'fellowship of the Holy Spirit'. The Church is a great leveller because it is the fellowship of those for whom Christ died, in which all have sinned and come short of the glory of God, and yet for all there is the possibility of the free gift of forgiveness. These are the badges and tokens of the fellowship in which the Holy Spirit freely, according to his will, distributes his gifts. And always those gifts are for the building up of the Body.

6. *'There should be no division in the Body'* (v. 25): Any jealousy concerning gifts given to individuals is destructive of the Body. We have witnessed this in recent times, in the inverted jealousy that has made some feel like second-class citizens because they lack the gifts, like speaking in tongues, given by the Spirit to others, who appear, and sadly in some cases feel themselves, to be superior.

As St Paul never tired of saying, such feelings have no place in the Church. Rather 'its parts should have equal concern for each other' (v. 25). Compassion, the particular virtue of Jesus which he has given to his Body, means that all are touched by the suffering of one; equally the joy of one can affect and infect all the others. Total sharing, not division, is the mark of the Body of Christ.

7. *In this Church, each member has a particular function to fulfil*. St Paul uses here the analogy of the human body with not a little humour (the mark of a good teacher!). 'The eye cannot say to the hand, "I don't need you!" And the head cannot say to the feet, "I don't need you!" On the contrary, those parts of the body that seem to be weaker are indispensable' (vv. 21–2). God has so

wonderfully created the human body that there is no division in it. All parts are necessary for the healthy functioning of the whole. All contribute to the 'miracle' that is the human being.

So also in the Church. *All* members, with the many and varied gifts they have been given, are vital to the life and well-being of the Body of Christ. In this way the Holy Spirit, coursing through the individual members in whom he is working his gifts, enlivens the whole Body of Christ. That he is the author and giver of life is true for each individual and true therefore for the Body, made up of the sum of the individuals. The distribution of the gifts by the Spirit ensures that no-one is left out, but that each member has a particular function to fulfil. This is a great encouragement to people who may not feel that they are gifted in the more obvious ways and may wonder whether they are able to 'help' at all. More will be said about this below, but let everyone rest assured that for *all* members of the Body of Christ there is a function – perhaps better a calling – to fulfil. 'Now you are the body of Christ, *and each one of you is part of it*' (v. 27).

We have now reached the point at which we are in a better position to answer the question. What has gone before is necessary background to the answer. Assuming it all as read, then we can say, Yes, certain people are given gifts of healing *within the context of the Body of Christ*. This is the normal way. Because we are members of His Body, Jesus relies on us now to do his work, proclaiming the Good News as he did, by preaching, teaching and healing. The good news for us is that he equips those he calls. And so first one member, then another, will be given a gift for a particular mission or situation. He never leaves himself without witness. The member allotted for a particular task is gifted to accomplish it.

I have said that this is the normal way, but the good Lord is not bound by his Church or his Sacraments. The Spirit blows where he wills, and sometimes we come across remarkable gifts *outside* the Church. This is very good for our humility, as the labourers found who had worked all day in the vineyard. I think of a story from the war, in which a young private soldier's compassion was used, for whenever he touched with his left hand a gaping wound, the flesh came together and it healed. Some people are greatly gifted for healing, but the true test is whether they give God the entire glory, asserting that *he* is the healer and not they themselves. When people claim to be 'healers', there is something in me that wants to give the glory to God by witnessing to them that it is the *Lord* who heals, and they have no power of themselves. As we say in the doxology of the Lord's Prayer, 'for *thine* is the Kingdom, the power and the glory . . .'

I hope enough has now been said to answer the second part of the question also. If we are members of Christ's body, the Church, and in a state of grace, then we are liable at any time to be 'gifted' to be Christ's hands in a particular situation. We may well be given one of the gifts of healing to further the Kingdom. Our task, as Jesus often told us, is therefore to 'watch', to be on the alert for when we are needed, to be open to the prompting of the Holy Spirit, who will tell us, if we are listening, when he needs us in a situation.

It is therefore of no consequence whether or not we *feel* especially gifted. As members of Christ we have the priceless gift of Christ himself within us, and there can be

51

no greater gift than that. And of course we are in that way equipped to help as his hands in the world, in any situation in which he requires us. It is an awesome privilege to be a member of Christ's Body here on earth. If we all realized (i.e. made real) our membership, and were alert to his bidding, the world would soon be at his feet, and God's Kingdom could be *realized* in a healed and 'whole' creation.

9

EVEN IF I DON'T FEEL
ESPECIALLY GIFTED,
AM I ABLE TO HELP?

I want to give an immediate answer in the affirmative to this question: Yes, of course you are! Unlikely as it may seem to us, God can, and wants to, use each one of us in his service.

Fortunately Christian service does not depend on our *feelings*! There must be very few of us who *feel* especially gifted. I doubt if anyone would dare to make such a claim. But if we pause for a moment in the Lord's pre-sence – and how vital it is to our spiritual life to have these times to pause and reflect each day, these oases of silence – we shall probably have to admit in all humility that there have been occasions when God has obviously used us in some small way to further his purposes of love. It would have been very surprising if we had felt at all gifted or equipped to meet the situation, but God supplied all our needs, the necessary grace, to see the matter through.

In the meantime we can all begin by listening, in our times of prayer, either with others or by ourselves, to what God wants to say to us. We should preface these opportunities to hear a word from the Lord by saying with Samuel, 'Speak, for your servant is listening' (1 Sam. 3.10), or with St Paul at his conversion, 'What shall I do, Lord?' (Acts 22.10). If we are alert we shall know what the Lord requires of us, and in what direction of service he will supply his gifts. It may be to persevere in prayer with others to undergird the whole ministry to the sick in our church or town. Gifts of prayer are needed more and more, as the Church widens its boundaries for ministry. Possibly we may be called into a ministry team in our church, usually after a long preparation of prayer. Or we may feel it right to go on one of the training courses in the healing ministry (see chapters 19 and 20). We shall need to talk to our parish priest or minister about all this, but we can all make a start on the road to being one of Christ's helpers by listening to his will for us in our times of prayer, and by reading the relevant literature about his ministry of healing (see the Book List, pp. 128–9).

Or perhaps our calling may be to serve much nearer home – to nurse or minister to a sick relative or neighbour. If we are found listening in our prayer, God will provide us with much to do and to be for him. And we can be assured that with the call he will provide the gifts and strength to perform his bidding 'for the building up of the Body of Christ'.

So don't rely too much on your feelings, but rather on your intuitive promptings. Search prayerfully for what God is calling you to do, and then go out and do it in his name and to his glory. There are many ways in which you can help to play your essential part in the forward move of God's Kingdom. Look around you, in your immediate vicinity, and you will find many needs close to you. Take up your cross with Jesus Christ and follow him in ministering to the crying needs of your fellow human beings. Remember that in ministering to them you also minister to *him* (Matt. 25.31–46). We shall be judged in the light of these acts of service that we have performed, or failed to perform – by whether we went to the help of someone in need, or failed to do so. He will supply all our need in the doing of it, and all theirs also. 'The one who calls you is faithful and he will do it' (1 Thess. 5.24).

10

WHAT SHOULD BE MY EXPECTATIONS WHEN I PRAY FOR MY OWN OR SOMEONE ELSE'S HEALING?

When a leader of a small prayer group was asked how he went about the difficult task of interceding for people before God in prayer, he replied:

> Whenever a person is brought before us with a need, we visualize that person in our minds as clearly as we can. We *think* of them. See them. See them in their sick or distressed condition. We do not dwell too much on their sickness nor try to 'feel' as they do. That would sabotage our effectiveness in building up a positive prayer approach. We think of them as they can be in God – well and whole.
>
> Next we focus our thoughts upon God. We think of his power, his goodness, his grace, his might, and when we have a clear picture in our minds of the sick one and of God we bring them *together* in the crucible of our believing hearts. We hold them there together as long as we can. We don't spend too much time particularizing our request (it is known anyway to God), but we concentrate more on becoming the channel between him and the needy person. Our ministry is to be a channel between his heart and theirs.[17]

It seems to me this Christian intercessor has got very many things right. He has caught the spirit of New

Testament teaching, indeed the spirit of Christ. He demonstrates his obedience to Jesus's teaching by engaging in intercession:

> Ask and it will be given to you; seek and you will find; knock and the door will be opened to you. For everyone who asks receives; he who seeks finds; and to him who knocks, the door will be opened. (Luke 11.9f.)

Then he engages in the act of intercession with his fellow Christians, again in obedience to Jesus's teaching:

> Again, I tell you that if two of you on earth agree about anything you ask for, it will be done for you by my Father in heaven. For where two or three come together in my name, there am I with them. (Matthew 18.19f.)

Moreover, that same prayer group leader is *positive* in his approach to God about the sick person. He does not dwell on the sickness or the symptoms, and so avoids the colourful details of a case history. This eliminates at once a negative element that too frequently saps the energy of our praying and destroys all expectations. Essentially we are praying, not for a man with cancer, for instance, but for a person whom Christ has redeemed and therefore wants whole. The intercessor is wholly right, when he thinks of the sick person, to think of him 'as he can be in God – well and whole'. At once this raises the level of expectation, which is going to improve our act of intercession.

Some people may say that it is wrong to raise expectations, as though whenever we engage in prayer we are seeking some magic formula to cure our own or another person's ills. But what we are seeking to do is to let God into the situation, for too often he is kept out of it by unbelief, or by a blind belief in the power of modern science, or a fear of the disease that cripples the will to fight it, or a reluctance to 'bring in religion as a last resort'. Far from it being wrong to raise expectations, it has always seemed to me that the Church too often fails to rise above zero in regard to expectant faith, and indeed prefers to lie down and take the punishment meted out. This is not the reason for which Christians are in business. As the Apostle tells us, we are 'a people belonging to God' in order to 'declare the praises of him who called' (us) 'out of darkness into his wonderful light' (1 Peter 2.9). God does actually will to call and protect us from the darkness of sin and sickness, so that we may follow his bidding in the wonderful light of wholeness in him. If we really believed this, we might be a deal more expectant in our praying.

Our interceding friend is therefore utterly wise in turning to the light and focusing his thoughts on God and on God's power, goodness, grace and might. The essence of expectant prayer is that it should be totally God-centred, God-focused. Much of our prayer fails, so that we become discouraged, thinking that we are never heard, simply because we focus either on the negative symptoms of the sick person, or on our own problems and deficiencies, instead of on God. The word intercession itself implies the presence of God, because it means that we take up our stance as a link between God and the person for whom we are interceding. And how right it is, as the climax of our intercession, to bring God and the sick person *'together in the crucible of our believing hearts'*. I love that phrase, which so perfectly describes the high peak of intercession and is full of expectation, for we hold them together in the crucible of our *believing* hearts. I repeat, our *believing* hearts, for perhaps herein lies the key to our approach, the map for our homing into the presence of God. The heart, the centre of our being, the place that should be Christ's glorious throne, this is the place of meeting, where our act of intercession is fulfilled. The holding together is not in the mind only; our faith must be more than cerebral. The Eastern Orthodox spiritual writers laid great emphasis on their discovery that true prayer consisted of standing before God in total attention *with the mind in the heart*. It is in this crucible of a believing heart that our acts of intercession are fired and refired, because *God is there*.

God's presence, eternally with us and within us, enables us to pray expectantly. I do not mean by this that we are to expect him immediately to do our bidding and fulfil our wishes. But expectantly we commit the whole person, or the whole situation, in need of healing, into the hands of a merciful and faithful Creator who knows his own plans and the destiny of each one of us. The writer to the Hebrews has a vibrant hope – 'an anchor for the soul, firm and secure' (Heb. 6.19) – in the presence of our 'great high priest who has gone through the heavens, Jesus the Son of God' (Heb. 4.14) who 'is able to save (heal) completely those who come to God through him, because he always lives to intercede for them' (Heb. 7.25). This is why he encourages us to 'approach the throne of grace with confidence, so that we may receive mercy and find *grace to help us in our time of need*' (Heb. 4.16). This is what we may pray for, expectantly and with utter confidence, for, as St Paul was told in answer to his earnest prayer for healing (which in his case did *not* result in a cure): 'My grace is sufficient for you, for my power is made perfect in weakness' (2 Cor. 12.9). Above all, the teaching of Jesus would have us high on expectancy: 'Ask and it will be given to you' (Luke 11.9).

What should I expect when I pray for healing?

I have emphasized the need for expectancy because I believe we have tended to be far too timid in that regard in our praying before the throne of grace. We should realize, as the hymnwriter has said,

> Thou art coming to a King,
> Great petitions with thee bring.

For since he *is* our King and our God, he knows our destiny and the destiny of the person for whom we pray. Like their Master, there are some people who seem in this life to be called to be made perfect through suffering. That is the mystery, a mystery which will only be revealed in the life of the world to come. Our humanness finds it hard to reconcile a belief in the God who wants us whole with what our eyes see in terms of suffering humanity.

We could say that this life is a crucible that fires us to render us fit and ready for the life of the world to come. Here we are in pilgrimage. Pilgrims have to suffer the hardships and rigours of the journey before they come to 'their desired haven' (Psalm 107.30). But their pilgrimage itself, their whole journey, is a prayer, a prayer for that wholeness known fully in the presence of God. Therefore they go on, knowing that on their pilgrimage there is 'no continuing city' for 'they are seeking one to come.' And they go on their way above all *expectantly*, knowing that God alone is the object of their search, and their ultimate destiny.

Our prayer for the sick is something like a pilgrimage, only we are doing the travelling on their behalf, while they are doing the suffering. So we go on expectantly, taking them in our heart as we go, knowing that the God who heals (Exod. 15.26) is the object of our search and of theirs, and that his is a love that will never let us go.

11

HOW SHOULD I PRAY
FOR A SICK PERSON?

My immediate answer, for a start, would be 'With others.' However, when Jesus taught his disciples to pray, he told them, 'go into your room, close the door and pray to your Father, who is unseen' (Matt. 6.6). The word he used for room means 'store-house' or 'shop'. Perhaps Jesus was using it figuratively, and telling them they needed to be like the householder who has treasures laid up – but spiritual treasures laid up in the heart, our inner chamber where we find God. The preparation for prayer is to quieten ourselves within. Jesus warned his disciples, 'do not keep on babbling, like pagans'. A spate of words will not gain us a hearing in the heavenly courts. Silence is the highway to God. Here are the preliminary steps, the vital preparations for storming the gates of heaven.

Only after this does Jesus give his instruction on prayer: 'This is how *you* should pray: Our Father in heaven . . .' (Matt. 6.9). We note at once that the pronoun 'you' is now in the plural. The fact that he assumes more than one will be engaged in the exercise is confirmed by the first word of the Lord's Prayer: it is '*Our* Father' to whom we are told to pray. There is much more strength in praying together, a lesson that Anglicans of my generation have been slow to learn, even though we have always acknowledged that the zenith of all prayer is when the Body of Christ meets together to celebrate the Eucharist. After all, we do have our Lord's own promise, 'Again, I tell you that if two of you on earth agree about anything you ask for, it will be done for you by my Father in heaven. For where two or three come together in my name, there am I with them' (Matt. 18. 19,20). The Greek actually says 'in the midst of them', or as George Bennett used to say, 'in the midstness'. When a group of Christians pray together, the power is there because Christ is in the centre. There is strength in numbers.

I should like to emphasize in every possible way the power of prayer when Christians are gathered together. This is an experience we need to undergo and believe in if we are going to be used in the ministry of healing. Offering to pray for someone is not much use unless we believe in the effectiveness of prayer! A personal reminiscence may illustrate the point I am trying to make.

Anne and I were on the way to visit Northern Ireland and Eire in 1984, and we stayed at the Rectory in Holyhead the night before we sailed. The priests had arranged a service of healing in the evening, and we had just reached the section of the service devoted to quiet prayer. The powerful silence was shattered by a noise that sounded as if Concorde was landing outside the porch. A person in motor-cycle gear and clothed in cameras entered, obviously in a hurry. The church-wardens did a noble job, in whispers of course, of quietening down the local press photographer, for that is who it was, and the 'Concorde' was of course his motor bike devoid of silencer. They assured him that his request for a quick photograph would be met in due course. He sat down in a back pew, first took off his cameras (a parson has a grandstand view of the congregation from the pulpit as well as vice versa) and then he shed his gear. By the end of the time of prayer he was on his knees. During the ministry in the next part of the service, he came up for a healing blessing. After the service he took a nice photograph of all of us who had been involved, and once more the Concorde sped into orbit, rather late for its next port of call.

A week later, one of the clergy met the photographer again and asked what had happened that night, saying he understood he had only come along for a quick photograph. 'So I did, but it was those people – those people at prayer. It was so powerful, I had to get on my knees and join them. Now I have invited Jesus Christ into my life and acknowledged him as my Saviour. I'm a Christian.' And so he is to this day. If ever I have a temptation to doubt the power of corporate prayer, I recall the photographer who 'touched down' that night in Holyhead and was himself touched by the healing hand of Christ.

So we pray for the sick person *together*, as fellow members of the Body of Christ. And so much the better if sometimes we do this in the course of a Eucharist, which, as one of our Anglican divines, Jeremy Taylor, declared, is 'the most powerful means of impetration (receiving what we pray for) known to man.' In this situation, just as in a simple prayer-meeting in a friend's front room or kitchen, there are many ways of offering the sick person in prayer to the healing Christ. Possibly the first essential is to be aware of the glory of Christ. Too often we come to the time of offering with our mind full of negatives, because we are concentrating too much on the disease. We pray 'for John with cancer', and too often the cancer comes first, John next and God, who alone can do anything about it, last. We must reverse this order. First, we enter the courts of heaven. We are coming to plead before the throne of grace. When Isaiah was praying in the Temple he was given a vision of the Temple filled with the presence of God. That is how to begin. Isaiah could then go on to converse with God *after* that, but the initial part of his prayer was a total awareness of God in glory, permeating the whole atmosphere, including his whole being. Every cell of his body seemed to vibrate with the glory of God. That is the beginning of true prayer. Of course we may not get our foot over the threshold of the heavenly courts every time we pray (God can *seem* a long way off at times), but prayer begins with a surrendering of ourselves into his presence. God present and permeating is paramount.

We respond to the Presence by being 'lost in wonder, love and praise'. And that may take a little time. Then we are gradually led to make our further offerings. After praise and thanksgiving may well come penitence, and then intercession – in this case our prayer for the sick person.

Intercession means standing in between the person and God, one of the most difficult forms of prayer. But there we are called to stand. The most quoted act of intercession in the New Testament is the occasion when four friends brought their paralysed friend to Jesus. That was their offering: their friend on a mattress, which they had to let down through the roof, after first breaking up the tiles until they made a large enough hole! They knew no other way of standing by their friend in the presence of Christ the Healer.

And intercession would be for us almost too difficult but for the Person who supremely moves in between – the Holy Spirit, the Go-Between God Himself: 'The Spirit helps us in our weakness. We do not know what we ought to pray, but the Spirit himself intercedes for us with groans that words cannot express. And he who searches our hearts knows the mind of the Spirit, because the Spirit intercedes for the saints in accordance with God's will' (Rom. 8.26, 27). The Spirit is not only the Author and the Giver of life, but also the great Intercessor.

The Holy Spirit is the Go-Between God who presides over our whole time of prayer, calling us into the presence, making us aware of the glory, lifting us in praise and thanksgiving, melting us in penitence and so making us strong to *stand in between* in our act of intercession. And as we stand between, let us not lose our awareness of the Presence, God permeating. We have brought our

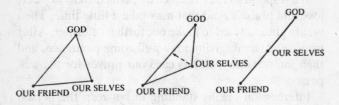

friend, the one whom we are offering specially before the throne of grace, but our concentration must be wholly on the God who alone has power to heal. If there has been a triangular situation, with God at the apex, our friend at the second angle and ourselves at the third, the object of our act of intercession is to straighten out (and so in fact to eliminate) our own angle, so that the triangle becomes a single line, on which we stand between God and our friend (see diagram above). George Bennett had a beautiful phrase to express his beginning and ending of intercession: 'dwell in the heavenlies'. Just *be* there, silently. Silence is the language of love and adoration. Another fine comment on this offering of intercession originated from George: 'We begin to pray when our prayer has ceased.' It is often in the afterglow of our praying, if we would only linger awhile in his presence, that the healing Christ communicates his will to us about those for whom we have prayed, or shows us a new vision. Loitering in his presence can lead to an experience of his power. That is the sick person's chief need, and an intercessor's part is to become the agent through whom that need is supplied.

12

WHAT IF NOTHING HAPPENS
AFTER PRAYER?

The first thing I want to say in reply to this question is that I firmly believe *all* prayer is answered. We have prayed to God who, as St Paul found out through experience, 'is able to do immeasurably more than all we ask or imagine, according to his power that is at work within us' (Eph. 3.20). If we believe in God at all it seems to me that we cannot help believing that he answers prayer. St Paul held this belief, despite his own experience about the 'thorn in the flesh' (see chapter 3). He was constantly encouraging his readers to pray, both by word (1 Thess. 5.17) and by deed (Col. 1.9) and never give up, as well as asking them to pray for him (2 Thess. 3.1). Would he have done this without a firm belief that God answers prayer? Would people continue to pray today if they thought God did not answer prayer?

It must be said, however, that God frequently answers our prayer in ways that we do not expect. He is full of surprises, and knows better than we do ourselves what is good for us, and what will contribute most positively to our ultimate destiny. If we fail to recognize this, we may well come to the conclusion that nothing is happening as a result of our prayer, and so we begin to despair. We think God is a long way off, that he cannot hear us, and ultimately that God does not exist.

This simply means that we have been looking in the wrong direction. Perhaps our prayer has been a shopping list of our wants and expectations, or of what we think God ought to do. Our expectations have probably been minimal and self-centred, because we fail to recognize how great God is. No wonder we are often disappointed about our prayers! Too often we remain on a human level, instead of allowing God to raise us up. That means we may not have truly prayed at all. We have remained in the centre of our own picture, without giving God room to get a look in. Our idea of God has been too small. No wonder we feel like dismissing the whole exercise, and saying that nothing has happened in response to our 'prayer'.

The first step in true prayer is to forget about our side of the picture and think only of God, and this goes for any kind of prayer – praise, intercession, thanksgiving, whatever. This is a way of getting ourselves tuned in to *his* will, by first realizing (i.e. making real) his presence. At first we shall require regular periods of silence in order to realize his presence within us. Then gradually we shall find ourselves able to create an interior silence, when tuning in to his will may become easier. But unremitting application and work is needed to achieve this. Henry Wadsworth Longfellow expressed it well:

> Let us, then, labour for an inward silence –
> An inward stillness and an inward healing;
> That perfect silence where the lips and heart
> Are still, and we no longer entertain
> Our own imperfect thoughts and vain opinions,
> But God alone speaks in us, and we wait
> In singleness of heart, that we may know
> His will, and in the silence of our spirits,
> That we may do His will, and do that only.

Once we begin to be tuned in to God's will, we shall find that things fall into place more easily. It will seem right to pray for some things and not for others. For some people we shall feel a real burden of prayer, and be led to concentrate on them, but perhaps not on others. We shall be given an instinct about all this, a gift of discernment, that will make our praying more orderly because it is ordered by God alone. I also suspect that we shall not so often be using that phrase, 'unanswered prayer'. We shall probably find that more things happen after prayer than we ever dreamed of. We shall discover what an exciting life it is in which God involves us, once we really start to pray.

Then, when someone for whom we have a great concern contracts a fatal disease, and when, although we have prayed for their healing, they die, rather than throwing up our hands in horror and saying that 'nothing happens', we may well find we can say something like this: 'Yes, I knew it. The time of their mortal destiny has been fulfilled; they have fought a good fight and finished their course; they have kept the faith and have a crown of righteousness in store for them (see 2 Tim. 4.7f); now was the time for God to heal them through death. "Thanks be to God! He gives us the victory through our Lord Jesus Christ." ' (1 Cor. 15.57.) What better eventuality could there be for the person, what more could happen, after our prayer? And if things don't work out for us just as we have hoped and expected, and we have to face grief and heartache, or disease and suffering, in ourselves or in others, then that also may be part of our spiritual pilgrimage, of our journey to wholeness.

13

IS THERE A DIFFERENCE
BETWEEN THE ANOINTING
AND THE LAYING ON
OF HANDS?

The Anointing is the name now more usually given to the sacramental means of grace that used to be called Holy Unction. The new title describes more simply what it is – the smearing with holy oil in the name of the Father, Son and Holy Spirit. The oil (pure olive oil) is holy because it has been blessed, either by the minister or, as in the Roman and Anglican Churches, by the bishop during a special celebration of the Eucharist on Maundy Thursday, to demonstrate the fact that it is the ministry of the whole Church that is being offered. The priest or minister anoints the patient by dipping his thumb in the phial or oil stock and signing him or her with the sign of the cross on the forehead, possibly on the palms of the hand (and sometimes, if attended by a nurse or doctor, on the dis-eased part of the body) in the name of the Holy Trinity.

The service of Anointing itself is brief and beautiful, though nowadays it is usually administered in the context of the Eucharist or one of the Offices. It is given at the time of the intercession, and includes the prayers of penitence. After the lesson, from James 5.14–16, prayer is offered, confession of sin is made and absolution is received. The Laying on of hands is then given (see below), followed by the Anointing. There should then be a period of silent thanksgiving before the final prayer

69

and blessing, if it is a separate service. In a Eucharist, the service is resumed at the Peace.[18]

There is no firm evidence as to whether Jesus himself used oil, but the name 'Christ' means 'the Anointed One', and we learn from Mark 6.13 that the disciples used it for anointing the sick, so we presume Jesus taught them to do so (perhaps by personal example). It is also interesting that when recounting the parable of the Good Samaritan Jesus described how he tended the wounds of the traveller by pouring in oil, a natural emollient, and wine, a good if primitive disinfectant. Anointing was of course an ancient act of consecration, used in Old Testament times, when priests and kings were anointed to consecrate them for their particular work. This still happens in the case of our own Sovereign during the coronation ceremony. The royal or priestly person is thereby set apart for God's service and work. The Anointing of the sick also can helpfully be seen as a consecration for a particular purpose, in this case the healing of soul and body.

I never cease to be amazed at the blessings which are given when the Anointing takes place.[19] I call it the Lord's 'deep-ray treatment', for it seems to reach to the joints and marrow, and above all to the heart of a person. Frequently it adjusts a person's equilibrium, enabling medical treatment to be given which had previously been impossible. And often, too, it brings about an inner healing, lifting a burden that may have been oppressing the person for decades, thus obviously leading to an improvement in health. Others feel a new strength and a commission to go on with their work and witness. Always there is the fruit of joy, and if not an immediate cure, certainly a new ability to cope with life.

The tradition in the Anglican Church has been to administer the Anointing only once during the course of a particular illness. But I have come to the conviction that really sick people need the spiritual resource to be kept at a continuously high level. After all, we should be surprised if a doctor told his patients to take only one dose of his medicine. I have therefore come to prescribe a frequent ministry of anointing in certain cases, for example, of cancer, motor neurone disease, multiple sclerosis and now, of course, A I D S. This seems to have been of help in the case of motor neurone disease, and I believe that we ought to err on the side of frequency, rather than deny a sick person a vital spiritual resource. I also hope we shall see this sacramental means of grace being administered to those in need of it on Sunday mornings together with the Holy Communion of our Lord's Body and Blood.

With regard to the preparation, I myself was taught that the confession of sin and receiving of absolution were essential to a right reception to this means of grace, and I still believe that a sincere preparation should be made as far as people's sickness will allow. However, I have come to see the rightness of George Bennett's teaching that forgiveness is a 'bonus' received in the sacramental grace of the Anointing, for according to the passage from James's Epistle which is the authority for this rite, 'The prayer offered in faith will make the sick person well; the Lord will raise him up. *If he has sinned, he will be forgiven*' (James 5.15).

In this context I feel led to quote part of a letter from a friend:

> I can't begin to tell you how I felt after receiving the sacrament (of Anointing). It was such a wonderful

71

experience there are just no words. . . . Don't hesitate to let anyone know the benefit of those who have experienced it. . . . One doesn't expect pain suddenly to go away, but it is the peace of mind which comes to one – all doubts and worries which had assumed such tremendous proportions have now just faded away, and the inward calm is something I just can't explain.[20]

And from a more recent 'patient':

I can never thank God enough for leading me to receive the Anointing and the joy in that experience for me was beyond all understanding, for I met Christ. It was the confirmation of the tiny grain of faith within me which gave much wonder and rejoicing. It fulfilled in me a longing to be sealed in the belief that healing of the mind and soul can be, and is, attained when the opportunity is given. As you anointed me I came to realize that God in his own wisdom was the one whom I should seek each hour for the next step. It gave me the courage and the vision so much needed to see the way ahead.

The Laying on of hands is also biblical, and as we have noted, is now part of the rite of Anointing. However, it is frequently used separately, because first and foremost it is an act of commissioning. Barnabas and Saul received the laying on of hands, after fasting and prayer, from the Church in Antioch, which thereby commissioned them for their first missionary tour (Acts 13.3, cf. Num. 8.10). Today the Church uses the same action with prayer to ordain and confirm, in other words to commission Christians to the specific office and task to which they are called. The laying on of hands was also an act of identification, as when a man laid his sins on the scapegoat (Lev. 16.20–22). In New Testament times Jesus used it in blessing (Matt. 19.13–15), and frequently for healing also (Mark 5.23; 6.6f; 7.32–4; 8.23–52). It was also used to impart the Holy Spirit (Acts 8.14–17). There is something of all this in the healing touch, but God is not bound to give particular blessings in response to particular acts. I often wondered what blessings and surprises God would have for a candidate when, as a bishop, I laid on hands in Confirmation, or when I laid on hands for healing. God is (mercifully) in charge, and the Holy Spirit blows where he lists.

Theologically there are many possibilities surrounding such an act, and since the rabbis used laying on of hands as a formal sign when 'adopting' their students for the next year's course of teaching, the idea of adoption as a child of God may also be inherent in it. Be that as it may, there is also a psychological significance to the act; touch, as the Churches seem to be discovering anew and belatedly, is a very meaningful act, as every mother and every lover should know. This is also being discovered anew (and belatedly) in medicine. An experiment in a hospital ward, where on the drug-round the nurses touched the patients on one side of the ward, and plumped up their pillows, etc., while on the other they made a coldly clinical distribution, showed conclusively that the health of the former improved more quickly. Again, the members of a certain General Practice decided to spend the first two minutes of each interview shaking their patient's hand, taking their coat, chatting about the kids and cricket, with surprisingly health-giving results. A little bit of T L C (tender loving care) is an old fashioned but effective prescription.

The Laying on of hands when used in conjunction with healing prayer, which may be silent or verbal, is a spiritual remedy of effective meaningfulness in the Christian Church. Probably used far more frequently than the Anointing, it has the same biblical background. The guidelines for its use offered by the United Reformed Church are:

1. that it should be ministered within the context of a worshipping Christian community, a prepared and praying people, open to the Holy Spirit;
2. that a Gospel proclamation or some statement should precede it;
3. that it should be a shared act of ordained and lay members.

I would add, that it be ministered with a woman and a doctor in the team, though of course this is not always possible. What is important is that the sick should be ministered to by means of the Laying on of hands with prayer, in order that we may in our generation fulfil the commission Christ gave to his disciples.

The traditional difference of emphasis between the Anointing and Laying on of hands has been that the Anointing is ministered less frequently, being reserved for more acute cases. For centuries it was used only as part of the last rites, but in 1967 the Roman Catholic Church made a welcome pronouncement, reinstating the Anointing as a sacrament of healing. In all Churches the Anointing is now used more frequently, and in the future we are likely to see even more use of oil in healing, because certain Churches are taking steps to authorize its use by the laity. After all, the use of olive oil as a remedy against many sicknesses in ancient times was extremely common.[21] Christians in the early Church may well have taken a drop or two of the holy oil from the sanctuary lamps, if a member of the family lay sick at

Are the Anointing and the Laying on of hands different?

home. Certainly a more frequent use would be welcomed today, and rather than maintaining any difference in emphasis, we may hope that the Anointing and Laying on of hands will be more often ministered together, as the Church prescribes.

14

ARE PUBLIC SERVICES OF HEALING A GOOD THING, OR DO THEY RAISE FALSE EXPECTATIONS?

A healing service is a non-liturgical service that has as its main focus prayer with the Laying on of hands. After an opening act of praise, in hymn and word, there are three basic components of such a service:

1. *The ministry of the word*. This will include a reading from Scripture, followed by an address of exposition or of some teaching about the Christian healing ministry. This is the great opportunity for biblical teaching in the service, which should not be missed. It is an occasion for the proclamation of the gospel of our Lord Jesus Christ.

2. *The prayer*. This is the central part of the service, and needs to be carefully prepared in such a way as to deepen the life of prayer for those who attend. Various forms of prayer may therefore be used, but the first essential is to allow people to have a true experience of the presence and power of God – which after all is the purpose of all prayer. Moments of silence should therefore be incorporated in order that God may have an opportunity to speak to each of those present. Thus there may be a conducted meditation, or a silent (yet corporate) saying of the Jesus Prayer, or a contemplative silence focused on a candle or the cross or water or some other evocative symbol. Usually there will then be an act of intercession (a standing before God on behalf of others), in which the congregation will be able to

mention aloud the names of any for whom they have a burden (but not the details of their illness!). Then all is offered up in the words of the Lord's Prayer, with a concentration that has 'the mind in the heart'.

3. *The ministry of laying on of hands*. This is the climax of the service, when those who wish come to the Communion rail for prayer and blessing. The team of ministrants will have prepared beforehand, both privately and corporately, to be open channels for the healing gifts Christ wills to give to his people through them. To be used in this way is a very great privilege, and such a call to minister must be approached in great humility. 'I am among you as one who serves', said the Master (Luke 22.27). How true it must be of us.

There will not, therefore, be a huge spate of words in the ministry. Counselling and giving advice is not appropriate at this point in the service. People have come to meet God, not to hear a sermon from one of his servants. Counselling may well be appropriate after the service, or at a time to be arranged later, but at this moment each person comes to be received by the Lord. The ministrant's part is not to be obtrusive, but rather to be sensitive to the Lord's leading concerning the word of prayer used. Often this will be given if the ministrant remains sensitive to the Lord's promptings. The ministry is a gentle thing, gentle in touch (Leslie Weatherhead always used to place his hands a fraction of an inch away from the head, barely touching, while George Bennett used to touch lightly the back of the neck and the left temple) and also gentle in word. The Lord's touch on the person's inner being is paramount.

Each person therefore who comes to receive the ministry also needs to be well-prepared. Penitence for our sins and faith in God's mercy are two helpmeets as we make the approach. If we want to describe our need in one short sentence, that can sometimes be helpful to the ministrant, but is not always necessary. Both need chiefly to fill their minds with God only and leave it all to him. 'The one who calls you is faithful and he will do it' (1 Thess. 5.24).

In answer, therefore, to the question, 'Are public services of healing a good thing?' we can say that they can be a very good thing indeed. They provide an opportunity to hear some good teaching; they enable one to progress in the life of prayer; they give one an experience of God's presence (though he is present with us always, and often when we feel him to be furthest away he is actually very near). And of course services provide an opportunity to receive the healing touch of Christ. Let us therefore not denigrate them too hastily.

Having said all this, there is one further factor to bear in mind. The state of affairs we long for is one in which the healing ministry is once again a normal part of the Church's liturgy and practice; when it will be quite usual to witness a healing blessing given, through anointing or laying on of hands or both, during the main celebration on a Sunday morning when the Body of Christ is gathered together and ready and eager to play its part as the praying Church. Mary will be able to ask the priest or minister beforehand for the anointing because she is to have an operation during the week, and in that prayer and blessing will be included not only Mary herself but also her family, fending for themselves at home and anxious for their mother, the surgeon and his team, the GP, the hospital chaplain and the nurses on the ward, who will all become part of the burden of prayer shouldered by that Church in the service and during the week. 'Carry each other's burdens, and in this way you will fulfil the law of Christ' (Gal. 6.2). Only so will the healing ministry be fully integrated into the life and witness of the Church.

The second part of the question, 'Do healing services raise false expectations?' is more difficult to answer, because people come with such a variety of different expectations, greater or less. I have often thought how many opportunities we miss through our *lack* of expectation! On the other hand, we should obviously be wrong to come expecting a display of magic, an instant cure at the wave of a wand.

What should be the object of the search for those who come to such a service? My answer, in a word, would be *God*, and him alone. I remember a doctor once saying to me that he could not believe in any healing ministry that did not redound to the glory of God. 'Thine be the glory' is truly the healing theme.

This will set the burden we bring, be it an anxious care or a cancer, in its true perspective. What is God saying to me at this moment of crisis in my life? – remembering that 'crisis' in Greek means 'judgement'. What stage of my earthly journey have I reached? Obviously a turning point, but turning to life or to death? Will it be a point of turning round in my tracks (i.e. a conversion)? If so there is hope in plenty. Or will it mean the same old life as before, merely increasing hopelessness? Here truly is a crisis, a time to judge and be judged, a time therefore for *metanoia* (with its original meaning 'change of mind') which we translate 'repentance'. Here in our crisis we can come face to face with God as we turn round to face *him*.

This is the sort of expectation to which I would want to point people, an expectation that transcends the immediate and perfectly natural desire for instant cure, and leads on to the eternal truths of God's love and his ultimate purpose for each of us.

The service will then be a time, an opportunity (the same word in the New Testament) for growth, an experience that will be of ultimate significance for our healing, whether in this life or the next. We are in his hands. There is no more hope-ful place to be.

15

HOW CAN WE HELP PEOPLE WITH SO-CALLED 'KILLER' DISEASES?

I assume this question refers to the most destructive diseases in the western world, heart disease and cancer. Now we have also to consider AIDS. With the warning that I am in the kindergarten concerning these very great personal problems confronting humanity, let us first tackle the word that has such an unholy power in our society – cancer.

Cancer could be seen as symbolic of our western lifestyle today. The greedy cancer cells become activated in the body and, unless prevented at an early stage, will eat away all the other good cells until the whole is destroyed. This is uncomfortably close to being a parable of contemporary human greed. The problem is that the disease, like the rain, falls on the just and unjust alike.

When cancer is diagnosed, people go through what psychiatrists call a psycho-social transition. At such a time their whole world view is re-assessed, as well as the part they themselves play in it, and this will involve major changes in the heartland of the self. Doctors recognize the openness of a person both to help and to harm at such times of crisis, and we may recall that the Chinese symbol for 'crisis' contains the elements both of danger and opportunity. It is a fact well-documented in clinical practice that such times afford an opportunity for growth as well as for reconciliation and change.

I should myself want to add to 'psycho-social' the

element of *spiritual* transition, for such situations afford the occasion and opportunity – perhaps for the very first time in a person's life – for assessing one's beliefs (or non-beliefs) and coming face to face with the ultimate things. Is there a God? Has he done this to me? Can he now help me? Sadly, and too frequently a hospital bed may provide the first opportunity its occupant has been given to face such major questions about human exist-ence. The immediate reaction in these situations will be one of fear, a nightmarish entering into a chasm from which there is no escape. The coming and going of white-coated professionals, who know what we don't, only increases the fear. The suspicion that one's family know too, and therefore must be grieving on the quiet, also increases the sense of isolation and near panic. And stress of this sort cannot be of help to anyone who is ill.

In this situation a sensitive Christian can be of tremendous support. I emphasize *sensitive*, because all bull-dozing and proselytizing are out, as they always should be. What is needed is a patient *listening* to the pain of the sufferer, and you first have to *be* that kind of sensitive listener, and be seen to be so, before anyone will trust you with their burden. The only preparation for a Christian who would fulfil this task is a long and faithful waiting upon, and listening to, God in prayer. Listening skills are of course a help, but it is only by the grace of God that we become able to be of use at such times, for it is *his* radiance the person needs to see reflected on our faces as they talk. *Mirrors of Love was* the title St Aelred of Rievaulx gave to his thesis on what it means to be a Christian. We are called to mirror the love of God to all with whom we have to do.

Such sensitivity – just being *there* when a person wants

to talk, sometimes giving them an embrace or holding their hand (for actions speak louder than words at these times) – can help in many ways. It can help to heal the hurts of the past as they come tumbling out, and a silent or spoken prayer for each situation, that Christ the Healer will reclaim it, will be a contribution to the total reconciliation and fulfilment. Many have progressed and achieved more in this part of their life than in any other, and a sensitive and humble Christian can be of great help as an enabler during this period.

Hospices have done a great deal for people in this situation. The wonderful work of Dame Cicely Saunders, who set out with the purpose of establishing such units as monuments 'to the enduring dignity of man', and of her many colleagues in the hospices, has put many in their debt, especially the patients who have been helped to fulfilment and peace. They have taught us what it is to care wholistically, especially in regard to the family. In one hospice I had the privilege of blessing a new wedding ring and taking a renewal of vows 'until death us do part', as the couple celebrated their silver wedding with the medical staff and other friends. The wife died a few days later, but a positive step had been taken in their relationship, and all was joy on that day, a happy memory for the widowed husband. Another blessing in Hospice treatment is that pain is kept under control, so that death when it comes can be faced without undue suffering and with dignity.

We also need to remember at this point that there is a power far greater than cancer, and that is the healing power of our Lord Jesus Christ. Too often the very word 'cancer' inflicts such fear and terror on a person's consciousness that the result is felt to be a foregone conclusion. This is far from the truth in the early stages of the disease. Medicine is having ever greater success in this area, and we can thank God for the skills of doctors and research analysts. There are also spiritual remedies that can be of great benefit in reversing the action of the cancer cells, which need to be fought against with all the weapons at the person's command. These spiritual remedies are a definite aid to fortifying the immune system.

Sometimes the disease is brought on by a great shock or loss, or by a wrong turning which has been taken in life. In the latter case, there needs to be repentance, perhaps after counselling, followed by a receiving of forgiveness and absolution. Sometimes there is also the need to forgive *oneself*. The Book of Common Prayer is right when it refers to 'the benefit of Absolution'. In a case of shock or loss – e.g. of a close relative, home or job – then Christian befriending is of very great help, especially if it leads to Christian faith and a regular receiving of the sacraments. I believe that in all cases of serious illness the spiritual temperature must be kept at a constant level, and I usually prescribe a very regular receiving of Holy Communion and frequent Anointing.

All of this I would also say in regard to AIDS, which for Christians is both a challenge and an opportunity to be met in Christ's name. There seems to be an instinctive conviction among us that the healing power of Jesus Christ is being shown to us again in this century to help in the fight against such serious diseases. At the moment we are fairly ignorant about AIDS; we can only have our suspicions of the pace at which it can escalate and of its terrible destruction of the immune system. But clearly all the resources given to the Christian Church must be brought into play. Possibly it is only these resources at present that can be of help. The day-to-day Christian befriending is of vital importance, as Jesus himself demonstrated in his healing ministry. He would go amongst *all* the sick, touching them and assuring them of the love of the heavenly Father. He was also very direct in his insistence that sin must be forsaken as he pronounced past sins forgiven. There is so much going away from God's laws in our generation that the rivers of forgiveness need to burst their banks and flow over us. The great *human* need in our time is for an injection of the *divine*, a massive conversion or turn-round back to God and a forsaking of 'the flesh pots of Egypt'. I certainly do not believe that God has 'sent' this disease – we must stop blaming God for everything. But I am inclined to think he will use it to bring back some sanity and love into the way we treat each other.

At the moment the massive aggrandisement of self on all sides in the world, especially in our northern half of it, needs a total negation, and, above all, forgiveness. The Churches must be unafraid in proclaiming the availability of this gift of healing for humankind. The conviction of sin and the ensuing 'benefit of Absolution' are two of the world's greatest needs today. These remedies, together with the constant love and support of the Christian community, the regular reception of Holy Communion and Anointing, are the powerful Christian weapons that will help the people who suffer from this terrible disease, and on a wider scale will gradually continue the process initiated by Christ on the Cross, of reconciling the world to God. This is what being a Christian is all about, for now this ministry is committed to us to carry out (2 Corinthians 5.18f). And this is why healing is being recognized again as such a vital element in the gospel (i.e. the good news) of our Lord Jesus Christ.

We must earnestly hope that, as research continues, medical science will bring most therapy forward into the preventive stage, and so be able to ward off many diseases before they take a hold on the body. A good example of this need for wise *pre*vention is heart disease. Most of us need educating about our style of life and the elements of daily living that bring on needless stress. Many probably know already that the experience of emotion takes place not only in our minds, but throughout our whole being. Such experiences as fear, anger and excitement result in hormones or body chemicals being released into the bloodstream in perfect balance according to the emotion experienced. For example, adrenalin, with its influence on the constriction and dilation of blood vessels, is the hormone mainly responsible for the symptoms of the 'fight or flight' reaction. Situations of challenge and effort raise the levels of adrenalin, while feelings of calmness and equanimity, especially when encouraged by a quiet prayerfulness, will actually reduce the adrenalin level.

Again, cortisol, one of the body's natural steroid hormones, regulates the fat, sugar and protein metabolism and exerts a measure of control on the immune system. While contentedness and well-being are more likely to ensure a normal level of cortisol in the body, the 'three D's' – defeat, distress and despair – will raise the level considerably. At a high level, the immune system is impaired, leaving one more open to infection and to cancerous disease. When regarded wholistically, it is doubtful if cortisol is of lasting benefit in resisting stress.

I use the word 'lasting' advisedly, because both adrenalin and cortisol are known as the stress hormones and are most influential in maintaining homeostasis. Homeostasis is the term used to describe the various functions of the body involved in maintaining a steady internal environment. The body has many mechanisms which can be brought into play to maintain such a balance. Distress and effort arouse the body hormones, and if this arousal is continued for any length of time it can obviously be dangerous, because the balance necessary for homeostasis can no longer be maintained. Symptoms of secondary stress such as exhaustion and burn-out are then likely to occur. The antidote is obviously alleviation of the distress and promotion of relaxation and feelings of wholeness and well-being.

Dr Peter Nixon, Consultant Cardiologist at Charing Cross Hospital, has been a pioneer in educating heart patients into a new way of life and explaining the concepts of healthy function and of its opposite, exhaustion. He has taught them – and the rest of us – that symptoms are not something to be suppressed by drugs, except perhaps in moments of crisis, but rather a prodding to which we must listen and hear and obey if we would learn to live with the strengths and limitations of our bodies. He has demonstrated this through his now famous 'Human Function Curve', which is reproduced overleaf with his permission.

Arousal is the degree of stimulation and effort we bring to whatever work we undertake, and Performance is the measure of how well the task is done. The forty-five-degree angle between these two signifies normal function, or, in Dr Nixon's words, 'the healthy individual working on the upslope has rapid, adaptable thought, comes up with original intuitive solutions, is vigorous, can take on extra problems without a shift in pace, and can maintain sustained effort'.

However, we are not as the Archangel Gabriel. Our bodies have limits, and if we push the arousal factor too

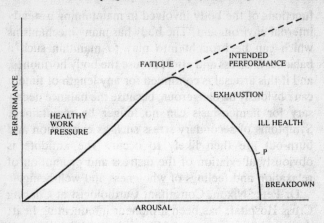

far the homeostasis mechanisms utter a cry of 'help'. If we then persist in making the effort, we go into the downward spiral which begins with fatigue and can end in ill-health and, if we pass the point of no return (P), breakdown. Of course we all have different thresholds, but once in the exhaustion bracket, the vicious circle of putting in more and more effort has to be broken by rest and recuperation if breakdown is to be avoided. At Charing Cross, Dr Nixon has devised the following checklist to help people discover why they have ended up on the downslope.

Because too much is demanded of me?
Because I cannot say 'no' when I should?
Because I am not sufficiently in control?
Because I can't cope?
Too angry, too intense, too upset, too irritable, too indignant?
Too many people – hassles?

Too many time pressures? Too impatient?

Because I am not sleeping *well* enough to keep well?

Because I am not keeping fit enough to stay well?

Because I am not balancing periods of hard effort with adequate sleep and relaxation?

Because I am out of real energy and am using sheer will-power to keep going?

Because I am infallible, indispensable, indestructible, immortal?!

We owe much to Dr Nixon's pioneering ways of re-educating us in how to reduce anxiety and tension, how to breathe well, and how to restructure our lives to include adequate rest and refreshment so that we ourselves may become a resource to others.

Another cardiologist who is concerned with this question, and has been in consultation with Dr Nixon, is Dr Herbert Benson from Harvard, who tells how he prescribes for his patients, so as to enable them to arrive at a state that is free from anxiety and more relaxed.[22] He has also made an extensive study of prayer and meditation techniques, amongst which he calls attention to four basic elements:

1. *A quiet environment*. Internal stimuli and external distractions must be 'turned off'. A quiet room or place of worship is a help.

2. *An object to dwell upon*. This may be a word, a picture or some symbol like a lighted candle. Concentration on one of these will help to clear the mind.

3. *A passive attitude*. This he regards as the most essential factor in eliciting the Relaxation Response. Thoughts and imagery, feelings and emotions may drift into one's awareness but should be allowed to pass on.

4. *A comfortable position*. The posture should be so

comfortable as to allow one to remain still for twenty minutes. Usually a sitting position is recommended.

Having pointed to the need for these four elements, Dr Benson then goes on to assess the patient's background and sensitivities, and to prescribe some kind of meditation or prayer. For our purpose here the most interesting, obviously, is what he would do for Christians. He has studied the teachings of St Augustine, *The Cloud of Unknowing*, Martin Luther, and Fray Francisco de Osuna, of St Teresa of Avila's *The Way to Perfection* (1562), and of the monks of Mount Athos. From these he has particularly learned the silent benefits of the Prayer of the Heart and the Jesus Prayer. I well remember his lecturing at Dr Nixon's first conference, and saying how he found that the slow repetition of the Jesus Prayer resonated perfectly with the steady heartbeats of a healthy person. For a Christian patient, therefore, he might well 'prescribe' the Jesus Prayer, to enable them to resonate 'with the music of heaven' and so be returned to health and well-being. Not for the first time have modern scientists felt a kinship with Christian mysticism.

These are some of the approaches through which doctors have pioneered ways of helping and alleviating the symptoms of serious diseases. It seems to me that the Church has lagged behind some of the more advanced doctors in applying spiritual helps and healing to the alleviation and overcoming of serious illness. Some doctors have pointed the way, as we have seen. The Church is possessed of a power beyond human telling, the healing power of the Lord Jesus Christ. As Cardinal Basil Hume told his monks in 1976, we as pastors have to learn to use that power, a power which can overcome such 'killer' diseases as we have been considering. The name of Jesus is far more powerful than the word 'cancer', though an outsider might be forgiven for not appreciating this from the way such matters are spoken of today. We must now show that the Holy Name also has the ascendancy over the term 'AIDS', before that too becomes an object of fear and terror which will plague the sensitive human mind and compound the illness. Let Christians return to a firm belief in the power of the Lord Jesus Christ, present to heal. Such belief was never more needed than in the dis-eased world of our time.

16

DOES THERE COME A TIME TO CEASE FROM PRAYER FOR HEALING?

Here I would re-iterate some of the things I said at the end of the last chapter. It is always right to pray, and to pray positively: 'the prayer offered in faith will make the sick person well' (James 5.15), and surely it is always right to pray for a person's *healing*. This positive power of prayer for healing is needed throughout all the Churches today. Such prayer may be too late to restore some individuals to perfect health in this life. For them healing may only be achieved in the life of the world to come – as indeed it may for us all: as my doctor in York used to say, in this life we are only healed into dying bodies. But let sickness and disease evoke a massive response of prayer from Christ's people today, let that prayer be offered ceaselessly with strong crying and tears night and day, and it could become a flood-tide of healing that would overcome our sicknesses and diseases. It could be the river 'from the throne of the Lamb' that flows down the middle of the streets of all our cities, to irrigate the trees whose leaves 'are for the healing of the nations' (Revelation 22.1, 2).

I have so far referred to the 'prayer for healing' which was how the question was phrased. I suspect, however, that many who ask this question refer to 'curing' rather than 'healing', that is, to situations where the medical prognosis is not encouraging and the patient is obviously dying, or preparing in thought to make the last journey in this life. More than ever in such situations prayer is needed, especially for ourselves as carers, that God will keep the door of our lips and give us true wisdom and loving compassion to help our friends in their final journey. All who minister at this crucial time should be covered by the Church at prayer. This will open up a new sensitivity to the whole situation and an ability to discern how best to pray and counsel.

My own hope would be for a complete openness with one another at such times, especially between members of a family, and more particularly between husband and wife. Frequently at such times the sick partner becomes the strong one, and is able to lead the thought and the prayer. It is essential for both to be surrendered to the Lord so that his wisdom and his love will take hold of them and lead them into a new depth of prayer – the experience of the nearer presence of the Lord who holds all souls in life. The prayer, if vocalized, will probably be centred on the healing of the life hereafter.

Complete surrender to Christ, with the sensitivity this brings, is essential at this time on the part of the helper (one of the offices St Paul mentions in 1 Corinthians 12.28), because there will come a time for the other to begin making the journey, a time beyond prayer when the first signs of the beatific vision are experienced. Many have asked their nearest and dearest to leave them at this time, so that they may fully experience the beauty of these moments of passing. At such a time the helper can only go to another room and give praise to God, thanking him upon every remembrance of the other, praising him for bringing the other to such a moment of blessedness, and commending the soul into the arms of a loving and faithful Creator, that it may rest in peace and rise in glory.

17

WHAT IS THE BEST WAY
TO DEAL WITH STRESS?

Many people think that a full life of work is stressful. There are indeed jobs which are extremely stressful, for instance manual jobs in industry where there is ceaseless noise, or work in difficult conditions underground. Work of this kind can undoubtedly shorten a person's life. There are also jobs in which moments of stress are inevitably encountered, for example Alastair Cooke in one of his brilliant letters from America quoted an airline pilot's description of his job as 'seven hours of boredom sandwiched in between two minutes of sheer panic'. On the whole, however, the actual work involved in our job is not the stressful part of it, but rather the conditions in which we work – bad relationships with fellow workers, or cramped and inconvenient environment, or the mad rush to get to work and get home again – these produce the stress points. What then is stress?

The most harmful type of stress is time stress. We get into our motor car, usually far too late and with insufficient time to make the journey, and drive *like hell* (in this case an expression all too appropriate) in order to arrive on schedule at the other end. The stress on our mind and heart, indeed on our whole body, is bound to be excessive, and seldom do we stop to think of the stress we cause on such journeys to other car drivers and their passengers, or to pedestrians. This is not only a stressful way of managing one's life, but also a sinful one, of which as Christians we should repent (i.e. turn around, away from)! Christians should be leaders in the campaign to keep stress *off* our roads. And of course time stress is experienced in many forms – meeting newspaper or publishers' schedules, stamping mail to catch the final post of the day in the office, getting the meals on time for a demanding family, and a hundred other ways. All this must add several points to our blood-pressure count, which is the body's way of dealing with such stress.

At this point we have to acknowledge that we *need* a certain amount of stress in our lives, in order to get motivated at all. Without certain pressures upon us we might not even bother to get out of bed in the morning! Without the necessity of providing for our family, we would not join the dole queue or search for a job (something that must put many under stress each week). Motivation to get on with our lives needs the stimulant of some stress. But the stress this question is about is the *needless* stress we inflict on ourselves and others.

A second type of needless stress is that caused by bad relationships. Sadly we see this phenomenon rearing its ugly head more and more often in family life. Unfaithfulness to the marriage vows, spurred on by a permissive attitude in society that condones rather than condemns such conduct, is responsible for much of the souring of relationships in family life. The lasting harm that it does to children, putting them under needless stress so early in life, is greater than we generally acknowledge, or than any social statistician can measure. We are gradually learning how deep are the scars imprinted on a young mind by such suffering.

Such stressful relationships may begin in the home, but of course are sadly continued wherever people meet. Little wonder that the Bible has so much to say about loving one another and living in harmony. The tension in our relationships with others is often a most harmful source of stress, and one which can become so detrimental to our life that it actually causes organic disease. When feelings of hatred and resentment are allowed to fester, the iron enters not only into the soul, but also into the body. Such stress can send our immune system and equilibrium off balance, and there ensues a situation of dis-ease. Most of such situations are avoidable, but sadly we ourselves create them by letting relationships turn sour. Stress of this nature is largely self-inflicted.

There is a third type of stress for which we are not always responsible, and that is stress created by circumstances over which we have no control, resulting from a hostile or noisy environment. Some situations in our inner cities are extremely stressful. The high-rise flat type of dwelling, which a generation ago was thought to be the panacea of the housing shortage, has turned into a nightmare in some areas, where vandalism by night and day has made many elderly people virtual prisoners in their own homes. Again, most of us at some time or another may have suffered from noisy and thoughtless neighbours. Here is yet another type of stress, this time usually inflicted from outside and therefore beyond our control.

Mercifully society is becoming aware of such stress points, and a more caring attitude in society is leading officialdom to tackle many of the social problems inherited from an age of speedy development in which projects were often given insufficient thought by the planners. There are many positive factors in today's society that contribute to people's well-being; and the Churches are increasingly playing their part in promoting the good of the city (the definition of politics) by standing with the under-privileged. While many people criticize the Churches for political involvement, we have to say that such involvement has nothing to do with *party* politics, but is totally humanitarian. The Fatherhood of God makes all humankind our brothers and sisters (St Francis would have said *all* creation). The Churches are increasingly conscious of their calling to be peacemakers, knowing that there has been committed to them the ministry of reconciliation (2 Cor. 5.19). Among other factors, I would mention the help that is given by the media through such programmes as 'That's Life', which can act as a preventive to mindless and heartless authorities riding roughshod over the poor and helpless. Our concern here, however, is what we as individuals do about preventable, *needless* stress.

Theodore Bovet, the Swiss psychiatrist, said that every human being needed to sit quietly in a chair for fifteen minutes every day. He inferred that such a period of relaxed, silent inactivity was vital to a person's well-being. Christian spirituality down the ages has advocated a 'quiet time' every day to be spent before God. Stress happens when there is pressure to live our lives at too fast a speed, to cram too many events into each day. It then becomes more and more essential to take some 'preventive medicine' by disciplining ourselves to have periods of quiet. Martin Luther once said, 'I am so busy, I cannot spend less than three hours a day in prayer'. When we hardly give ourselves time enough to think, how do we know our life is going in the right direction, or is being lived according to the will of our Creator, or is of any use at all to our fellow human beings?

To keep this more relaxed lifestyle, to which doctors are pointing us, in trim, and so to eliminate needless stress from our lives, may mean a complete turn-around (the actual meaning of conversion) from our present behaviour. It will mean a gradual tackling of many stress points – the way we drive a car, the way we rush off in the mornings without much thought of God, the corners we cut in our dealings with others, the image we project of being too busy to deal with the concerns of others which don't interest us, the subjects on which we are touchy and on which we know others are – and so on. But the essential question is how to build up our inner being and character so as to be able to deal with them.

I don't know of any better way than a quiet orienting of the day each morning, a time of quiet when, as the Eastern Orthodox spiritual writers would tell us, we give ourselves space and time to stand with our mind in our heart before God. This is not solely an intellectual exercise; our mind is hyperactive all day in any case. It involves the mind quietening itself by dwelling in the heart, the seat of the emotions and centre of our being, *before God*. Here is the beginning of the journey within, which will give depth and meaning to our life's pilgrimage. Orthodox spirituality recommends that such stillness should be accompanied by the slow and rhythmic saying of the Jesus prayer: 'Lord Jesus Christ, Son of God, have mercy on me.' Some people, on the other hand, will at times need total silence, stillness and solitude. Others will need to 'search the Scriptures', using one of the many aids to Bible study such as the Bible Reading Fellowship notes or William Barclay's commentaries on the New Testament. Others again will need an 'icon' on which to focus their quiet gaze, a lighted candle or a crucifix. Yet others will need the aid of a book, while all of us may need any of these aids to the spiritual life at one time or another. It is good to have variety for the spiritual as well as the physical digestion.

What is the best way to deal with stress?

If we want to give ourselves a chance of remedying the needless stress points in our lives, then some form of quiet or contemplative prayer is essential at the beginning of each day, in order to give direction and meaning to our being and doing on that day, and so gradually to eliminate the needless stress and confusion from our lives. We shall be led to work at difficult relationships, realizing the flash points, and being more open with people, if necessary going through the matters that cause hurt in order to come to a partnership together with the Lord and thus with each other. We shall be led to a better timing and ordering of our day, starting earlier on our journeys and giving ourselves space in the diary. (I have learned from Anne who gives herself space at the sink before cooking, that I need to gain space on my desk before I write or engage in study!)

This will lead to a recollection of the Lord's presence at different times of the day, a time, only a moment possibly, when we are able to recall or re-collect the period of quiet we enjoyed at the beginning of the day and the message or text of Scripture we gleaned from it. This may be at the canonical hours of prayer – 3, 6, 9 and 12, or when the clock strikes, or before we begin a new occupation or take a journey. A *recollectedness* will lead to a *collectedness* in life and so help to eliminate the stress that mars our lives so needlessly. And that is another way of saying, we need God and a consciousness of his Presence within and around us.

18

HOW DOES THE MEDICAL PROFESSION REACT TO THE CHURCH'S MINISTRY OF HEALING?

I suppose all good doctors have always had what we now call a wholistic outlook about their ministry. I recall the old family doctor sitting on the bed and having a chat, and though one might be feeling rather ill, his visit was invariably a tonic in itself. Of course he had not been wasting his time. He had asked some perceptive questions about attitudes and animosities, possibly even resentments and fears, and had tried to allay any feeling of dis-ease in these areas. He had also given some sound advice and encouragement, and probably shared a good laugh. All this was powerful therapy, probably more potent, in fact, than the coloured water that seemed to be a usual prescription in those days (though this did at least look more interesting than a modern drug in tablet form!).

All this was part of the art of healing, which modern scientific method and the increase in patient and case loads seems to have relegated to secondary importance. Mercifully, however, most general practices are now looking at this problem, and there is once again a far more open attitude to the totality of a patient's needs. Doctors increasingly have a wholistic attitude in practising health care. For instance, when a patient is under stress they are no longer satisfied to prescribe endless tranquillizers. They seek to ascertain the cause of that stress by asking the patient about the family situation, work or relationships.

In this present climate therefore, where the patient is truly treated as a person, doctors almost invariably welcome a ministry of compassion and care by the local church. They also on the whole welcome a ministry of prayer – even for themselves! I know of one parish where it was decided that each member of the congregation should write a letter to their own GP at St Luke's-tide (when Christians specially remember the medical profession), to say 'Thank you' for the ministry of healing they had received during the year, and to give assurance of a regular remembrance in prayer. That was a healing act in itself! And of course doctors will be only too glad if the local Christians are praying for one or more of their patients. Doctors are clever people, and they know that spiritual well-being in a patient will help to bring about physical recovery. They also know that a living faith in God is a vital element in the fight against illness and disease.

Many doctors do in fact pray for their patients, some-times silently – non-verbal prayer is just as effective – and sometimes overtly if the doctor knows the patient shares the same Christian faith. One doctor I know is part of a praying group himself, and if his patients are willing and give permission, he takes them to the group for prayer and counselling. The benefit here is that a member of the praying group who 'resonates' with the patient can then be assigned to offer on-going care.

In one west country town, the central practice of six doctors has invited the clergy to staff the afternoon surgery sessions, so that patients who seek spiritual help or counselling can then be referred to them. One of the doctors and one of the priests are planning to work out a

101

model together for closer co-operation between doctor and priest. In a midland town a consultant psychiatrist, after a year's study of the Christian healing ministry at university, plans to set up a Christian healing resource centre where distressed and depressed people may come for consultation. And in a midland city a hospital chaplain who is both doctor and priest, and his lay assistant, work in partnership in integrating the medical, spiritual and caring resources of the area; in speaking to many groups, medical and lay; in bringing doctor-and-clergy groups together; in planning a day centre of Christian healing; and in assisting at conferences at the interface between the Church and Medicine. Another doctor, once a consultant haematologist, now works full time in the Christian healing ministry, together with his wife who was a health visitor. Indeed, many medical directors of hospices, consultants and general practitioners, not to mention the nursing profession and other professional and ancillary staff, are now speaking and writing openly of the key contribution of their Christian faith to their clinical practice.

There are also institutions actively promoting closer co-operation. The foundation of Dorothy Kerin at Burrswood near Tunbridge Wells is one where deep Christian faith undergirds the work of clinical medicine. The Church of Christ the Healer, dedicated by Bishop Cuthbert Bardsley in 1962 a year before Dorothy Kerin died, is both focus and inspiration of the life and work of that place. As we saw earlier, Dorothy Kerin herself laid the foundations in the community, and in the hearts of its members and of people the world over, through a vibrant faith in the healing touch of Christ and in his love for all who come to him. She herself had been miraculously healed from a mortal sickness fifty years previously.

How does the medical profession react?

Here in her community today the partnership of the Church and the medical profession goes from strength to strength, as all patients are treated by the medical staff and chaplain working side by side. The director is a young doctor whose Christian faith and medical expertise are harmonized together in one 'offering' of wholistic care. He would be the first to say that his whole team is imbued with the same pastoral spirit. The combination of drugs and anointing with holy oil is a normal prescription which demonstrates the equal care of the whole patient.

These, you may well say, are surely exceptions, and you may be right. But I believe there is an increasing willingness by Church and medical profession to work together. Sometimes it is the Church which lags behind in the persons of its clergy. Sometimes it is Medicine, in the persons of traditional doctors. But there is a growing number of instances of communication transcending the traditional Church/Medicine divide, and this will increase provided that our theological colleges take the Christian healing ministry into their curriculum and that the medical schools and teaching hospitals similarly turn their attention to spiritual factors in health and disease.

There have been many agencies in the field which have tried to bridge the divide. The Guild of Health, founded in 1904, was first in the field. Other Guilds and Fellowships followed, including the Institute of Religion and Medicine (IRM) in more recent times. It was for this purpose that in 1944 William Temple founded the Churches' Council for Health and Healing, which today has representatives from the BMA and from the Colleges training in all the main branches of medical science, as well as from all the Christian Churches. At the moment it is engaged in an on-going working party with the Royal College of General Practitioners.

The Acorn Christian Healing Trust has also been taking some new initiatives in the last few years. Pairs of Christians, one with a medical training, are being encouraged to serve as a sign of the coming together of Church and Medicine in their area by taking initiatives such as joint gatherings for dialogue and teaching. The Christian Listeners movement, too, has as one of its primary purposes the bringing together of the work of the Church and Medicine, by getting local doctors and clergy to co-operate in selecting and monitoring the training of the Listeners (chosen from groups of prayerful Christians). They will then use the Listeners in the local situation to assist them with their case-loads. This will be a half-way house, as it were, between a befriending service and full-scale counselling.

Another resource in this field is Caring Professions Concern (CPC), which seeks 'to encourage and challenge Christian professionals in the caring professions to live for Christ in the power of the Holy Spirit in their everyday lives, to act as a prophetic voice in the caring professions and to train caring professionals to minister to the whole-person needs.' From this alone it will be seen that doctors and their colleagues are becoming more open to a 'wholeness' ministry in Christ.[23]

Another good sign is that doctors and other caring professionals are increasingly being used in the day-to-day ministry of the Churches, particularly at healing services. Doctors, nurses, physiotherapists and others are continually 'Laying on hands' in the treatment of their patients, so it seems totally natural to find them in a team of ministers laying on hands during a service of healing, or during a Communion service in which a healing ministry is offered. Personally I feel it adds a necessary dimension to such a team, and at a service of anointing I like to be accompanied by a doctor to demonstrate the wholeness of the ministry.

Some people may think that patterns may change in a multi-faith and multi-racial society. They may, but there are signs of encouragement for Christians. I know of one Hindu Practice in London which regularly sends patients to the local Christian Church, and tells them sometimes that that is where they ought to be! The Muslims also have a profound respect for a holy man, and a priest or minister who is found to be practising a healing ministry among his congregation is likely to gain their co-operation and support. The best contribution that we as Christians can make to this new, emerging society is to be found fully expressing our faith in the Lord Jesus Christ by obeying his commission to heal in his name, and by practising a wholistic teaching and healing ministry. If we do this, we shall gain the co-operation of doctors of all faiths and none. And more than this: we shall by God's grace be making a tiny contribution to the healing of the nations, and so to the coming of God's Kingdom and the healing of creation.

19

WHAT RESOURCES FOR CHRISTIAN HEALING ARE BEING PROVIDED BY THE CHURCHES?

The immediate answer is that there is such a plethora of resources that it is hard to find one's way about – though no doubt some readers will claim that nothing has been heard about it in *their* Church. So where do we begin?

The main resource for healing is the practice of the presence of God. Where God is worshipped in word and sacrament there is a resource for healing. Healing comes in the context of praise. We can truly assert that the gospel sacraments are healing sacraments, that Christ is present in power as the child is born again in the water of Baptism or as the pilgrim partakes of Holy Communion; and again, that the hearing of the word of God in Scripture or when it is preached is an occasion of healing. All these are times when the Christ who heals is present and provides a resource (we could say, a resurrection) for his people. So we can also say that when the Church goes about its main function – the worship of Almighty God – it is providing a resource for healing, though teaching is needed to enable Christians to *realize* this fact. For Christ is true to his promise, that he is present to two or three gathered together in his name, and his presence is healing.

The first point we would stress, therefore, is that the basic equipment and function of the Church is therapeutic. The priest or minister when administering the sacraments or preaching the word is providing a resource of Christian healing. Sermons often provide material for jokes, and send some people to sleep (which may itself be therapeutic!), but it is not unknown for people to receive healing during a proclamation of the word, or during the reception of a sacrament. This is particularly true of the therapeutic sacraments of Absolution and Anointing. The release given after a Confession, when the words of Absolution are pronounced and the person actually experiences a freedom from the weight of sin and the burden of anxiety it causes, is so therapeutic that a new state of well-being and wholeness is usually the immediate result. As we have seen, the Anointing with oil, too, is specifically focused on the healing of the whole person in body, mind and spirit, and is accompanied by the laying on of hands and the forgiveness of sins. Little wonder, then, that so many healings follow the administration of this sacrament. Thus the Church has always been equipped with plenty of resources for offering the healing blessings of Christ to his people. As Leslie Weatherhead once remarked, the only tragedy is that so much grace goes unappropriated.

The Churches have also set up specific agencies to promote the resources for Christian healing. As mentioned in an earlier chapter, six months before he died in 1944, William Temple set up the Council of Healing, now the *Churches' Council for Health and Healing* (CCHH), whose office is at St Marylebone Parish Church, Marylebone Road, London, NW1 5LT. It has a wide membership including all the Christian Churches, the medical profession through its specialist colleges and the BMA, all the healing guilds and fellowships, homes and resource centres, as well as other agencies of Christian healing. The Council acts as the 'umbrella' organization and agent of communication between all who are involved in the work of Christian healing; and its remit includes the promotion of sound teaching on the subject, of co-operation between the Church and the medical profession, and of prayer for healing nationally.

Most of the Council's member bodies are of earlier foundation, and here I would list in particular the agencies, guilds and fellowships which provide resources, or encourage the Churches to provide resources, for Christian healing. The first in the field was the *Guild of Health*, founded in 1904 by Dr Percy Dearmer, Conrad Noel and others to encourage co-operation between the Church and the medical profession. Its purposes include enabling the study of 'the interaction between physical, mental and emotional factors in wellbeing, and their relationship with the spiritual life in prayer and meditation.' The headquarters of the Guild are at Edward Wilson House, 26 Queen Anne Street, London, W1M 9LB.

The following year James Moore Hickson founded the Guild of Emmanuel, which in 1933 became the *Divine Healing Mission*. From the beginning it was based in prayer, with the conviction that the healing of the Church itself was a priority. In 1917 Hickson experienced a call to proclaim Christ as the Healing Saviour throughout the world. His work is carried on today by the Mission, which has its headquarters at The Old Rectory, Crowhurst, Nr Battle, East Sussex, TN33 9AD. People may come and stay there for periods of a week (for preference), to rest and receive ministry in a context of daily worship. Excellent courses of teaching in the healing ministry are also run for clergy and laity, and there are regular healing services, open to everyone. The director of the Mission also goes out to parishes to run training seminars and missions.

The Guild of St Raphael was founded in 1915 specifically for Anglicans, and like the CCHH has its office at St Marylebone Parish Church. Its emphasis is on the sacramental aspect of healing, and it has branches in the parishes all over England and abroad.

Each of these three Guilds issues a quarterly publication: that of the Guild of St Raphael is *Chrism*, while the Guild of Health publishes *Way of Life* and the Divine Healing Mission *Abundant Life*.

Yet another fellowship to have its office at St Marylebone is *The Institute of Religion and Medicine* (IRM), which as its name implies is dedicated to bringing together the Churches and the caring professions, and which works through field groups in various localities.

Similar to the IRM, but specifically for Christians in the caring professions is *Caring Professions Concern* (CPC), with its office at 34A Hilltop Road, Earley, Reading RG6 1DB. It provides training courses, literature and videos that are relevant to Christian professionals, and aims to challenge them 'to live for Christ in the power of the Holy Spirit in their everyday lives'. Another aim is 'to act as a prophetic voice to the caring professions on ethical issues'.

The *Acorn Christian Healing Trust* (Acorn), founded to support our own ministry, also has the aim of blending the work of the Churches with that of the caring professions, and providing orthodox teaching and training in the Christian healing ministry. Acorn now has a resource centre where books, tapes (audio and video) and other materials on the healing ministry are available, together with expert advice. The Acorn Trust office and the centre are both at the same address: Whitehill Chase, High Street, Bordon, Hampshire GU35 0AP.

In addition to the resource centre the two major

109

projects launched to further the aims of Acorn are the 'Apostolate' and 'Christian Listeners'. Founded in 1984, the Apostolate, as its title implies, consists of pairs of committed and praying Christians, one member in each pair having a medical training, who will act as signs in their locality of the coming together of the Churches and the caring professions, and take initiatives to bring this about, as well as helping to provide teaching and training in the Christian healing ministry. Christian Listeners are also men and women of prayer, who are jointly selected by the local doctor/clergy fellowship, trained to a certain standard of attentive listening under the supervision of a member of the Acorn staff who has pioneered this training, finally selected again by the doctor/clergy group and then used by them to assist with their case loads. The Acorn staff have produced training manuals as resource material for both Apostolate members and Christian Listeners. An Executive Officer has recently been appointed to assist in developing the Acorn work.

The healing homes also provide a rich resource of Christian healing. *Burrswood* (Groombridge, Nr Tunbridge Wells T N 3 9 P Y) was founded by Dorothy Kerin after the last war. One of her last acts was to witness the dedication of the fine church of Christ the Healer there. Today there is a fully staffed nursing home under medical supervision – the director is also a doctor – with a chaplaincy team, and a place to stay, Chapel House, named after Dorothy Kerin's place of pioneering work in Ealing. Many children now use the facilities as there is a remedial swimming pool. There are also healing services each day over every week-end, open to all. With a staff of seventy, Burrswood is the largest of the Christian healing homes and resource centres.

I have already mentioned Crowhurst and Whitehill

Chase, but before we continue our journey along the south of England moving westwards, let us take a trip to London, where the *London Healing Mission* fulfils a growing need at 20 Dawson Place, London, W2 4TL. The Reverend William Wood gave his life to the work here, and now the mission continues its expanding work under the present missioner and his wife. Healing services are held on Thursdays, morning and evening. Also in London, at the address previously mentioned, the *St Marylebone Healing and Counselling Centre* has recently been opened by the Prince of Wales. A doctor's surgery, music therapy rooms and other facilities of Christian therapy are sited in the crypt of this parish church.

Let us now take the old 'Bournemouth Belle' and travel down to *Green Pastures*, 17 Burton Road, Branksome Park, Bournemouth, B H13 6DT, a most pleasant and welcoming home of healing, of Methodist foundation. With thirty-four beds, there is ample room to stay and enjoy the delightful surroundings as well as receiving ministry.

Just outside Bournemouth in the Wimborne Circuit of the Methodist Church is *Crowe Hill*, now looked after by the ex-wardens of Green Pastures. A Christian worship centre in the country for renewal and healing, it is much used for day retreats and conferences, and is a counselling and therapy centre.

A little further into Dorset lies the *Post Green Pastoral Centre* at 56 Dorchester Road, Lytchett Minster, Poole, Dorset, B H16 6JE, part of the Post Green Community founded by Tom and Faith Lees. The Centre ensures by good organization that the caring, healing and teaching ministry pioneered by the community will continue, providing training, teaching and supervision.

Further west still we come to *Whatcombe House*, yet another community, founded by Reg East as a healing resource centre of teaching and fellowship. Regular courses are held on the Christian Healing Ministry.

Progressing further still into Dorset, we come to the *Pilsdon Community*, Pilsdon, by Bridport, Dorset. Founded by Percy and Gaynor Smith in 1958, it is now under the direction of an ex-chaplain of Charterhouse, and provides a haven of support for the vulnerable and those whose lives have been under heavy stress. Pilsdon owes much to the inspiration of the Little Gidding community, with its routine set by a daily round of prayer.

As we move into Devon we find a similar project at *Venton Manor*, near Totnes. Under the supervision of a doctor it takes twelve young people at a time with a view to healing and rehabilitation. Crossing into Cornwall we complete our tour of the south and west with the *Trelowarren Fellowship*, Marogan-in-Meneage, near Helston, TR12 6AD. Founded in 1974 to deepen spiritual awareness generally and promote the healing ministry of the Church, this is an ecumenical fellowship with an ancient chapel now dedicated to St Luke and St Cecilia (it concentrates on art therapy also), which has a fine library and accommodation for up to thirty.

As we return along the north Devon coast we must pause at *Lee Abbey*, a large house in a majestic setting near the top of the cliffs, run by a young and yet mature Christian community, a place of pilgrimage for hundreds, especially in the summer months. Renewed by the Spirit the community is a resource of healing, and frequent seminars are held on the Christian Healing Ministry.

In Somerset, too, much is going forward in the Name of the Christ who heals. Bath and Wells diocese was the first to appoint a full time adviser on the ministry, and there are other ministries officially authorized by the bishop. There is also the *Ammerdown Centre* in the grounds of Lord Hylton's home just outside Radstock. A Roman Catholic foundation, it is thoroughly ecumenical and holds courses and seminars on many aspects of the Christian healing ministry, especially concerning the healing of society. There is also a link here with *Maranatha* which we shall mention later on.

As we progress up England we pause outside Cirencester at *Harnhill Manor*. Founded in 1986, this Christian Healing Centre came out of prayer and the devoted ministry of Arthur Dodds in the Cotswolds. Housed in a peaceful old English manor house, with the church lying adjacent, it is run by a small community with a priest as leader. This new foundation provides a welcome resource for that part of the country, where people can stay and conferences are held. As in all the centres, prayer is made a priority.

We must not miss out Wales on our tour, where at *Ffald-y-Brenin*, Pontfaen, Fishguard, Dyfed, SA65 9UA, farm buildings on a south-facing hillside, with wonderful views over the wooded Gwaun Valley and the rolling Preseli Hills beyond, have been transformed into a self-catering Christian retreat, especially for members of the caring professions.

Travelling on to the north-west of England we come to *Ellel Grange*, near Lancaster, close to the M6. After a vision undimmed for eight years of a Christian healing centre in this area, the founder and his colleagues came to Ellel Grange in 1987. Again the whole project – and the finance – came through prayer, and its ministry team is now in constant demand as people come from far and wide.

Crossing the Pennines into Wensleydale and pausing at *Scargill, Kettlewell*, sister to Lee Abbey, on the way, we eventually arrive at *Spennithorne Hall*, near Leyburn, North Yorkshire, DL8 5PR, opened by the Archbishop of York in 1982. Here again is a haven of peace where a small number of people can stay, and as in all the centres, take part in the daily round of worship and the weekly healing service. It has a fine setting in glorious countryside, with therapeutic air! The small staff has a priest as resident leader. Further south, near Doncaster, there is the *Manor House Project*, 11 Hillcrest Road, Wheatley Hills, Doncaster, DN2 5ND, while on the Lincolnshire coast there is a small Christian healing home for guests who need refreshment and ministry, at *Christ Home*, 21 Queen's Parade, Cleethorpes, S. Humberside, DN35 0DF. All these homes and resource centres are brought together annually by the CCHH in a conference for their leaders.

There are of course many other resources for the Christian healing ministry. Of the growing number of these I would mention an organization in Essex in which doctors, nurses, priests and laity are involved called *The other ministry of health* (Dr Geoffrey Clarke, 89 Warren Road, Wanstead, London E11 2LU); the *St Barnabas Counselling Centre* in Norwich; *The Society of Mary and Martha* (Dr Sarah Horsman), Sheldon, Dunsford, Exeter, EX6 7LE; *The Pennal 'Whole-person' Clinic*, Pennal Rectory, Machynlleth, Powys, SY20 9JS, *Care and Counsel*, St Mary Magdalene Church, Holloway Road, London N7; and the *Pin Mill Christian Healing Fellowship* c/o Kirton Rectory, Ipswich, Suffolk, IP10 0PT. The various *diocesan retreat houses*, too, are places of refreshment and peace where increasingly conferences on Christian healing are held; while many people find peace and healing with the *St Julian's Community*, Coolham, Horsham, W. Sussex, RH13 8QL.

Besides these many organizations there are also the centres of pilgrimage, where Christian healing is being increasingly experienced – *Walsingham* in England and *Haddington* in Scotland; and a new community of Roman Catholic and Methodist foundation called *Maranatha* (Westway, Western Road, Flixton, Urmston, Manchester, M31 3LE), mainly dedicated to national healing, though personal healing is regularly experienced at their conferences. There is also the only extant shrine of healing in England at *St Wite's Church and well* in Whitchurch Canonicorum, near Bridport in Dorset, to which the Acorn Christian Healing Trust made pilgrimage in 1986.

In addition to the normal healing ministry offered in the course of their day-to-day pastoral care, the Churches are now organizing themselves to co-ordinate this care and ministry and render it more effective. It may come as a surprise that the *Church of Ireland* has been 'organized' in this regard since 1932, having a head start on the English Churches. In that year, following a visit of James Moore Hickson, a Warden of Healing was appointed to oversee the work in the Church of Ireland, and a centre was established at St Andrew's Church in Suffolk St, Dublin, where a festival of healing is held annually to coincide with the meeting of the Synod. There are now also centres in Belfast and Derry. Noel Waring was the first warden and laid the foundations of the ministry in Ireland, a work that has in more recent times been carried on by Stanley Baird and Jim Farrar. This ministry has always had the support and leadership of the primates and bishops.

The leadership of the Churches in England has also

been active. The *Baptist* Churches have a central health and healing advisory group, pioneered by Dr Stanley Thomas. The *Methodist* Conference has appointed a minister to oversee the work, and it was he and other colleagues who produced the excellent Methodist workbook on Christian Healing called *In search of health and wholeness*. The *United Reformed Church* has given especially strong leadership to Christian healing, and has produced three excellent teaching and training kits. The pioneer in this work is now the chairman of CCHH. The *Roman Catholic Church* is again giving a lead since the decree of 1967 restoring the Anointing as a sacrament of healing. The *Anglican* bishops have sought to forward the Church's healing ministry at the Lambeth Conferences in this century, and most of them now have an adviser in the ministry to co-ordinate the work in the diocese. The Archbishops also have an adviser. In all Anglican and Roman Catholic dioceses, too, the oils are blessed in the rites of Maundy Thursday, thus providing a vast sacramental source of healing for God's people.

So there are plenty of opportunities and resources. Let us pray that they will be fully appropriated.

20

HOW CAN I PREPARE
MYSELF TO BE USED IN
THE CHRISTIAN HEALING
MINISTRY?

Personal reminiscences can be very boring, but I think I can best begin to answer this interesting question by telling what happened to Anne and myself. What some of us know as the Acorn vision was born out of a listening to God over a prolonged period. This is hard to do in the pace of life today, but mercifully we were sent on a sabbatical by a wise Archbishop who obviously discerned that we needed such space. I know he would have agreed to a saying which is now our conviction: 'The greater the pace, the more the space' – the more, that is, one's *need* for space. We may recall again Luther's remark that he was so busy, he could not function on less than three hours' prayer a day. Anyway, gratefully we went off on our sabbatical.

We had planned it *religiously* by setting ourselves a reading schedule, so we went equipped with a suitcase of books. And we set about our task with vigour, until we both had an overwhelming conviction that the Lord was saying to us, 'Now shut those books and listen to me for a change.' We had *thought* that was what we had been doing, but it was obviously time – we recalled that in the New Testament the word for 'time' is used to mean *God's* time, or the right time or opportunity – for us to do some honest listening to him, to make sure we were going his way, not our own. So we put the books down and looked up and listened, and for part of each day we walked in Ashdown Forest where the views are extensive. We did little else for three weeks, and the 'little else' has become one of the most important things we were led to do in our lives. How thankful we were to be given the grace of obedience in order to respond to 'the Voice'. For out of that opportunity for listening came a clarity and a certainty of what we had to do.

I am telling all this because the first thing I want to say in answer to this question is about listening to God. It is only natural that in the phrenetic rush of life today, our prayer time and opportunity for space to be quiet can become skimped and formal. From time to time it needs an overhaul. So we go on Retreat or take a break on our own. I want to suggest that to prepare for this ministry we may need more than an overhaul; more of a complete rebuilding. Our spiritual life (I know it is unwholistic to compartmentalize our life, but one has to have a way in and this is the right direction) has to become a vibrant listening to God, dreaming dreams and seeing (his) visions, so that we know where we are going. We so easily get lost in the maze of life today, that we need to climb up on the helpful bridge and view the whole landscape in order to see the way – the Way, *his* Way – in which he wants to lead us. All our lives – and the life of the Church as a whole – would acquire a greater usefulness if we would only set out on any course of action after first really listening to the Lord's bidding.

I therefore want to plead with you that on your quest you will first enter the school of listening, by ensuring that your quiet time is rebuilt on listening lines. You may well need some prolonged space in your routine in order to effect this, so be bold enough to change your routine and prayer methods if you envision a better way. Ensure also that your life is fed by spiritual writers; often God will speak directly to our hearts in this way. A friend who is a hospital chaplain recently wrote to tell me of his joy in receiving students from a theological college as members of his chaplaincy team. He gives them essential reading in the techniques of the Christian healing ministry. And because he is alarmed by their lack of wider reading, he also encourages them to extend their interest among the works of the spiritual writers and theologians – Mother Julian, Jean-Pierre de Caussade, Carlo Carretto, Teilhard de Chardin, John Nicholas Grou, Hans Küng, etc. I would add such contemporaries as Michael Ramsey, Basil Hume, Robert Faricy, Henri Nouwen, Jürgen Moltmann, Morton Kelsey, Bernard Häring, Kenneth Leech and Jean Vanier. And I would again say, Give yourselves space.

A good example to follow in this has been set by the young visionaries of Medjugorje, who have given themselves space to listen to our Lady speaking to them. Soon after the visions began in 1981 she asked them to form themselves into a prayer group, and promised to guide them. She asked of them three hours prayer each day, saying, 'Do not be surprised because I ask for so much prayer, but you are weak because you pray too little'. She also asked for fasting twice a week. During this period she told them not to choose a vocation, and not to marry or go into a convent. Their priest asked through one of them why they should not even go into a convent. Our Lady's reply is significant for each one of us: 'The most important thing for all Christians is to enter into the depth of prayer; only then can one make the right choice'. As the priest commented, spiritual life consists in the deepening of prayer, and the elements of this deepening are to pray more, to fast and to love. Our

Lady gave them further advice: 'If you want to be very happy, live a simple, humble life, pray a great deal, and do not delve into your problems but allow God to resolve them'.

This is of great significance for those of us called to serve others in the ministry of healing, and indeed for all of us who bear Christ's name. Life has become more and more complicated, with the development of advanced techniques. We have even made the Church complicated, and the same is true of theology – and of therapy. The result is that we have become problem-centred. We pray about someone's cancer, instead of desiring Christ with all our being for the suffering *person*. We put ourselves in the centre, wanting to be the guides instead of allowing God to guide us. Words and advice can lead us (and those we seek to help) away from God. We need instead to concentrate on the heart, and listen to the voice within. That is true prayer. And a simple, humble life, with a great deal of prayer, is the paving-stone of the road to true happiness: not delving into our problems, but refusing to be consumed by them every minute of the day and allowing God to resolve them is a word of healing from our Lady of Medjugorje for our time. If there is a lesson the Church of this generation needs to take on board, it is 'Let go, let God'. We all need to *trust* him, to learn the meaning of the Lord's assurance to St Paul, 'My grace is sufficient for you, for my power is made perfect in weakness.' And an essential preparation for this ministry is to make sure we learn to put a foot forward in perfect trust in the God who heals and saves, without any reliance on human resources. We should remember that Jesus led his disciples to launch out into the deep and to place total reliance on him. A prayer of admission of our total inadequacy – 'Lord, I am out of my depth' – may be the beginning of true prayer and total trust. In the deep we realize our need for his grace and undergirding and sustaining help, for in the deep we are confronted by our own total inadequacy. Only when we have been humbled by such a realization, does God come to communicate with us and mould us into the vessels, albeit of earthenware, through which he is able to carry out the work he has destined us to do. Until we have been taught by such an experience to hang on his every word, we shall remain in ignorance of what the destiny is that he calls us in faith to fulfil.

'Prayer introduces the human spirit into God's realm where the rock of life dwells' said Theophan the Recluse. The first essential is to make the pilgrimage thus far, before we proceed to learning technical details about the healing ministry. As a great preacher used to say, 'It only takes me a short time to prepare my sermons but it takes me a lifetime to prepare myself'. This is true also of anyone who feels called to minister Christian healing. Dorothy Kerin spent seventeen years under disciplined preparation after her healing before she opened, and began her ministry at, Chapel House, Ealing. And every day's work also had some hours of prayerful preparation. We cannot build an edifice of such stability in a hurry. So let us give ourselves space; time for God.

Our life of prayer is of course assisted and advanced by our studies concerning the ministry, just as our studies need to be undergirded by prayer, something too frequently forgotten today. In the Orthodox Church a theologian is first and foremost a man of prayer. Together with my colleagues on the Acorn staff I have pondered long on what are the essentials for a training in the Christian healing ministry. Underlining all I have so far tried to say, it is obviously important that we should experience for ourselves and study the sacraments of healing – Baptism, the Eucharist, Anointing, Laying on of hands, Absolution. If Baptism is the primary healing sacrament in which we are healed from our birth trauma by being born again into Christ and his Body, the Church, then the Eucharist is the ongoing sacrament of healing for the Christian pilgrim, which preserves his body and soul unto eternal life. Bernard Häring has this to say concerning the Eucharist:

> In Christ and in the Church, the Eucharist is the central and most fruitful sacrament of the saving/healing grace of God. It is also a principal sign of 'forgiveness of sins', of healing hurt memories, a source of peace and an energizing resource for the peace-mission of all Christians. The Eucharist is an efficacious sign of healing faith, hope and love that enables the community and each believer to radiate wholeness and peace, to serve the poor, to care for the sick and to heal the depressed and the anguished. When rightly celebrated, it communicates that joy in the Lord which is a source of strength and health.[24]

As Michael Ramsey has said, Christ is there 'in His timeless potency'. We also need to learn about the Anointing and Laying on of hands (see chapter 13); and about Absolution and the healing properties it conveys through the assurance of forgiveness.

Contrition, repentance and absolution enable our growth as persons. And even the wounds we receive on our life-journey can be used by God as he seeks through Christ to make us 'a new creation' (2 Cor. 5.17), so that through our proclamation of the gospel and ministry 'we may present everyone perfect in Christ' (Col. 1.28). Our destiny is 'to be conformed to the likeness of his Son' (Rom. 8.29). Just as we grow in our body, so we must grow in our mind and emotions, in our spiritual life, and our relationships. For much of this growth we need the help of others, from our parents and onwards in all relationships. Particularly we need the 'grace of our Lord Jesus Christ, the love of God and the fellowship of the Holy Spirit' (2 Cor. 13.14). A continual growth towards wholeness of being should be the object of our search and of all our training.

Relationships are one of the main sources of such growth, and certainly the four major relationships of our life as Christians (Stephen Neill's quartet) – God, my neighbour, myself and creation – are formative. It is essential to have good relationships in all of these.

How do we view God? For our view will determine the mode of our relationship. Is he truly our loving Father – the God and Father of our Lord Jesus Christ, the God who heals and saves and inspires, the one God, Father, Son and Holy Spirit? Our relationship with him is forged through worship, prayer and reading the Scriptures. Such things must take priority in our lives.

And who is our neighbour? When an expert in the law asked Jesus that question (Luke 10.29) he received an unexpected answer. His neighbour was to be the person he had been brought up to despise and ignore – the Samaritan. What kind of relationship do we have with people – with our colleagues at work, with friends, physical neighbours, relations? Do we love them as ourselves? Can we at least give thanks for them?

And who am I? What kind of relationship have I with myself? Have I, like the Prodigal, come to myself? Or have I just got on with the rush of life and not bothered about my own personhood and its growth? I am made in the image of God, and the unity of my personhood is made up of my body, mind and spirit. Is each part, as well as the whole, treated in a healthy way? I am also a Christian, a person who is incorporated into the Body of Christ, and so acknowledge him as its Head, not only as my own Saviour and Lord. Life in relationship takes on another dimension because of this fact, a fact to which I have to relate constantly as I consider and come to my true self.

Finally, for our health and well-being our relationship with creation and the natural order is important. After a horticultural therapist had been working in a mental hospital for some time, enabling the patients to be aware of the seasons by having their own little piece of garden, the doctors were able to say that the general health level in the hospital had noticeably improved. An awareness of creation gives us an enhanced awareness of the Creator God. Indeed physicists today are making us aware of the interrelatedness and interconnectedness of all creation. They have shown how each elementary particle is not an independently existing unity but a set of relationships reaching outward to form other relationships. Again, a pair of electrons which have had a relationship, even though separated eventually by light years in space will maintain that resonance with each other. Relationship is a vital element within all God's creation! So let us not be shy about talking (as most of us do) to animals and birds and plants. St Francis had a most healthy relationship in this respect.

For all these relationships to be maintained in good health, we need resources. Part of our training – for life and not just for this ministry – will be to ensure as Christians that these are also received regularly to maintain that healthy condition. The first Christians realized this at an early stage in the Church's development. We read in Acts 2.42 how they settled on four essentials as a basic and necessary rule:

> They devoted themselves to the apostles' teaching and to the fellowship, to the breaking of bread and to prayer.

All trades and professions see that their members receive in-service training and are kept up to date with new knowledge. This should be an obligation for Christians too, as we seek to purvey the good news of Jesus Christ to each new generation. As we have seen, the healing resource centres run courses in this ministry, for instance a one night a week type (St Marylebone Healing and Counselling Centre) or a week's residential course (The Old Rectory, Crowhurst, in East Sussex or Ellel Grange, near Lancaster). Such resources may also increasingly be found in the local Churches, often at deanery or circuit level. We all need to engage in ongoing teaching. Obviously the fellowship of other Christians is also vital to our well-being, fellowship that begins in the regular breaking of bread and reaches outward in various activities during the week; while the prayer, as we have seen above, is the rock on which this whole ministry is founded.

The hope must be that such training will enhance in us the ever-deepening sensitivity which is so needful for the ministry of healing, a sensitivity to what God is saying in each situation, as well as to those we are seeking to help. Those of us privileged to engage in this ministry know full well that his grace is always sufficient for us and that his power is made perfect in weakness (see Corinthians 12.9). The essential factor for us all is so to prepare that we put ourselves in the way of that 'amazing grace'.

Notes

1. W. Foerster, quoted by John Wilkinson in *Health and Healing*, to whose researches I am indebted.
2. John Wilkinson, op. cit.
3. See Book List.
4. M. Maddocks, *The Christian Healing Ministry* (SPCK 1981), pp. 9, 10.
5. Ibid., p. 13.
6. Quoted by Selwyn Hughes in *God wants you whole* (Kingsway Publications 1984) where he describes DNA.
7. See *The Christian Healing Ministry*, Part 1.
8. See Arthur Bryant, *Set in a Silver Sea* (Collins 1984), p. 114.
9. In his book *Healing Miracles* (see Book List), ch. 4.
10. In his book *Power Evangelism* (Hodder & Stoughton 1985), p. 46.
11. Available at £16 post free from the Acorn Trust Office, Whitehill Chase, High Street, Bordon, Hants, GU35 0AP.
12. *The Christian Healing Ministry*, pp. 118f.
13. Dorothy Kerin's account of her healing appears in her book *The Living Touch*, available from Burrswood, Groombridge, Nr Tunbridge Wells, TN3 9PY.
14. In *Praying for Inner Healing*. See Book List.
15. In his book *The Healing Power of the Sacraments* (Redemptionist Publications 1984), ch. 6.
16. His book *Healing the Family Tree* (see Book List)

126

offers many new insights into the whole realm of inner healing.

17. Selwyn Hughes, op. cit., pp. 85f.
18. See *Ministry to the Sick*, Authorised Alternative Services, jointly published by the publishers of *The Alternative Service Book 1980*.
19. I have given some instances in *The Christian Healing Ministry* (see Book List), especially pp. 116ff.
20. Ibid., p. 121.
21. See Thomas Häberle osb, *Helping and Healing*. Sheldon Press 1986.
22. In his book *The Relaxation Response* (Fount Paperbacks 1976), pp. 78ff.
23. For fuller details about the resources mentioned here, see chapter 19.
24. In *Healing and Revealing* (see Book List), p. 58.

A Short Book List

Bennett, George, *Miracle at Crowhurst*. Arthur James 1970.
— *The Heart of Healing*. Arthur James 1971.
— *In His Healing Steps*. Arthur James 1976.
— *Commissioned to Heal*. Arthur James 1979.
  The distillation of his teaching by this pioneer in the healing ministry.
Cosslett, Neil, *His Healing Hands*. Marshall Morgan and Scott Publications Ltd 1987. Basic teaching.
Duncan, Denis, *Health and Healing: A Ministry to Wholeness*. The St Andrew Press 1988. An exposition of the healing ministry by the one-time Director of the Church's Council for Health and Healing.
England, Ann, ed., *We Believe in Healing*. Highland Books 1986. Thirteen witnesses to Christ's power to heal today.
Faricy, Robert, SJ, *Praying for Inner Healing*. SCM Press 1986. A book 'to help you to pray for your own inner healing'.
Frost, Raphael, OSB, *Christ and Wholeness*. James Clarke 1985. A historical and theological plea for the restoration of the healing ministry.
Gardner, Rex, *Healing Miracles: A Doctor Investigates*. Darton, Longman & Todd 1986. A well-researched source book for the signs of our times.
Gunstone, John, *The Lord is our Healer*. Hodder & Stoughton 1986. A useful textbook in a small format.

A short book list

Hamel Cooke, Christopher, *Health is for God*. Arthur James 1986. By the founder of the St Marylebone Healing and Counselling Centre.

Häring, Bernard, CSSR, *Healing and Revealing*. St Paul Publications 1984. A guide to healing based on sound spirituality.

Kerin, Dorothy, *The Living Touch*. First published 1914. Burrswood.

— *Fulfilling*. Hodder & Stoughton 1965.

The writings of a saintly mystic who pioneered the healing ministry and founded Burrswood.

McAll, Kenneth, *Healing the Family Tree*. Sheldon Press 1982. The ministry of a remarkable doctor.

MacNutt, Francis, *Healing*. Ave Maria Press 1975.

— *The Power to Heal*. Ave Maria Press 1977.

— *The Prayer that Heals*. Hodder & Stoughton 1982.

A best-selling author with a worldwide ministry.

Maddocks, Morris, *The Christian Healing Ministry*. SPCK 1981. A standard textbook for study.

— *Journey to Wholeness*. Triangle 1986. The journey model of healing.

— *A Healing House of Prayer*. Hodder & Stoughton 1987. Prayers for each day of the month and special seasons. A book for the time of prayer, private and public.

Wilkinson, John, *Health and Healing*. The Handsel Press 1980. Excellent resource for the biblical material.